CIDER AND MORE BESIDES

Esmond Bulmer

CIDER AND MORE BESIDES

by

ESMOND BULMER

The Memoir Club

© Esmond Bulmer 2010

First published in 2010 by
The Memoir Club
Arya House
Langley Park
Durham
DH7 9XE
Tel: 0191 373 5660
Email: memoirclub@msn.com

British Library Cataloguing in
Publication Data.
A catalogue record for this book
is available from the
British Library

ISBN: 978-1-84104-510-8

Typeset by TW Typesetting, Plymouth, Devon
Printed by The Amadeus Press, Ezra House, Cleckheaton BD19 4TQ

For the family

Contents

Foreword

Esmond Bulmer describes how the Bulmer family built the world's largest cider company over more than a century. As an MP between 1974 and 1987 he saw at first hand how little those in politics and those in industry understood each other. He left the House of Commons to chair the company until he retired. He describes how the world in which he was brought up of patriotism, a paternalistic approach to employees, the moral teaching of the Church of England, a gentlemanly approach to the rules of capitalism and respect for authority all fell apart; how the failure of the political class to understand and to foster the creation of wealth in an increasingly competitive world led to decline which sometimes appears inexorable; how Britain's failure to define its relationship with Europe has frustrated the creation of a new political settlement and how the media, with its relentless concentration on the short term, frustrates the long term strategies on which our prosperity, and perhaps in a global context, even man's survival on the earth ultimately depends.

Prologue

Time, like an ever rolling stream
Bears all its sons away;
They fly forgotten, as a dream
Dies at the opening day.

Isaac Watts, The Psalms of David Imitated

So we sang on the last day of term. The Rugby of my day was rooted in the Arnold tradition of muscular Christianity and in the concept of duty hugely reinforced by World War.

My prep school had been evacuated to the middle of Dartmoor. As a boy of nine, on the eve of D-day, I was taken up to the top of Crocken Tor by the headmaster to be told that my father had been killed – the tears flew on the wind and down the years. Life was transient and death was certain.

As an adolescent groping my way from the mediaeval cosmic drama of heaven and hell to the world of reason I came early to question the nature of free will. I remember staying up to the small hours in a sixth form group with Spencer Leeson, then Bishop of Peterborough but previously headmaster of Winchester, debating its limitations. As I pass my three score years and ten, it has become ever clearer to me that heredity and environment have forged me beyond my knowing.

Before the creation of a successful family business, my forebears had been priests, soldiers and landowners in the north of England where they had risen against Henry VIII in support of Rome. This had proved to be an expensive mistake.

After school I spent my National Service in the Scots Guards. Although on standby for Suez, I never saw action but learnt much about life from those who had. The need to live for the moment was for many the lesson of war but assumed a very different complexion when I went to live in Rome where *la dolce vita* was challenging the heirs of St Peter.

As a boy I had spent holidays in County Kerry fishing and regularly met Derek Warlock then Secretary to Cardinal Griffin and latterly Archbishop of Liverpool. He sensed that I was struggling with a vocation and suggested that before I went up to Cambridge I might like to spend time in Rome. I accepted his invitation and together with a friend, Richard Gridley, who was going up to Oxford to read Greats, duly appeared at students' lodgings in the Via della Scrofa just behind the Piazza Navona where we were housed under the roof and all too close to the church bells across the street. The building was in fact a *palazzo* where the *piano nobile* was home to a Cardinal whose Cadillac swept into the courtyard just as we arrived. The porter saluted as he passed and then spat. We must have looked surprised – he pointed to the number plate: SCV which he translated as '*Se Christo videsse*, 'If only Christ could see'. The tension between the sacred and the profane runs deep in the history of Rome as we became increasingly aware.

Our tutor was one of four priests responsible for keeping the Latin language up to date; he had great good humour but no intellectual curiosity – the bombus atomicus was a divine mystery. We attended lectures in Latin at the Gregorian University while learning Italian at the Berlitz. After the usual lunch of a bowl of pasta and a litre of rough wine the two merged all too easily. This routine compared unfavourably with other attractions of the post-war capital of which there were so many. An old family friend who had been in our Embassy before the war introduced us to the Roman comedy of manners and explained the tensions between the old nobility and the new, the fascists and the communists and the hidden world of the mafia and the church. The experiences of the war had tested so many family relationships – sometimes to death. To be taken out to be shot without knowing who had betrayed you happened all too often throughout German- and Russian-occupied Europe but in Rome such memories might be buried in *la dolce vita*.

I remember one lunch party where John had invited the head of one of the great Roman families who, he told me, had a wife in Italy, a wife in Switzerland and a wife in America and children by all of them, together with his current girlfriend. Also invited was the Cardinal whose title was 'Keeper of Latin Morals'. The girlfriend was at most twenty, at least forty years younger than the Prince, dressed by Ungaro and of *bella figura*. She swept in, panned the assembled company and, going up to John, pecked him on the cheek and said, 'My dear John, I am so sorry, I have come on the wrong day' and disappeared. Italians have style. Protestant guilt is alien to their culture. The beautiful life is to be lived to the full on stage – and in bed.

John told me that he had been playing golf with Ciano, the Italian Foreign Minister, in 1940 and Ciano had told him that Mussolini was going to declare war on Britain the next week. The next day a tax inspector appeared on his doorstep to suggest that they might come to an accommodation. John told him that he did not see any merit in the proposal since Italy was about to declare war on Britain, to which the tax inspector replied, '*La guerra, la guerra, non diciamo di cose si triste,*' 'The war, the war, let us not talk of anything so sad.' Nothing, not even war, must be taken too seriously.

Rome opened my eyes and my ears. The fruits of the Grand Tour are writ large in many of our great country houses and sowed in me the passion for collecting which has been a huge pleasure in my life.

Although I cannot sing a note the first time that I heard Renata Tebaldi and Tito Gobbi sing *Tosca* I knew that I had entered another eldorado. That all art aspires to music and that the deepest feelings are best expressed through it is true for many people.

In the Ascent of Man to turn the other cheek and treat your neighbour as yourself was a turning point. Tragically such simple precepts became subsumed in the struggle between men for earthly supremacy and the history of the Church is more often stained by blood than elevated by love. To its critics the Church of Rome was the ultimate protection racket. To its supporters it still retains the keys to the kingdom.

Returning from Italy I went up to King's College, Cambridge where many of my family had been before me. At the age of twenty-two I appreciated the opportunities of university far more than I would have done if I had gone straight from school. I read history on the basis of the proposition that you would have a better chance of knowing where you might be headed if you had some idea of from where you had come. The Tripos was broadly based: English history, the history of Europe and the ancient world, the history of political thought and the Principles of Economics. My father, who had also been at Kings, read economics and had Keynes as his tutor. Years later after I had become a Member of Parliament I used to think if only we could have compared our experience across the generations: I could have explored his recollections of Keynes' account of the evolution of monetary theory and his fears of the consequences of the Treaty of Versailles – both pivotal to an understanding of the history of the twentieth century. Much of the pleasure and benefit of university is to debate with friends issues across the spectrum of life and from myriad exchanges to try to plot one's own course.

I had fallen in love and knew that I wanted to get married. I was not going to be a priest but Lord Halifax's jibe, 'Scratch a politician and underneath you will find either a parson or a bookie' raised a smile when I read it. I had been attracted to the Foreign Office but was persuaded by my uncle to join the family business. Years later Adrian Cadbury, who had also been at King's, told me that he had been summoned by his great uncle to be told that as he was the best of the bunch he would join the company and his first job would be to sort out the family.

CHAPTER 1

Why Cider?

WHY CIDER? My great-grandfather was Rector of Credenhill for more than half a century. Like many a country parson he had time to devote to his hobbies. A predecessor had been Thomas Treherne, author of *Centuries of Meditation*, one of the greatest of Anglican mystical writings, but my great-grandfather was no mystic and found much comfort in the study of roses and cider apples.

Cider was the *vin de pays* of Herefordshire as it was of Normandy and Brittany and both in large part owed this inheritance to the monastic orders. Throughout the second half of the seventeenth century and much of the eighteenth, it was unpatriotic to drink wine formerly provided by our maritime and continental adversaries. Lord Scudamore was the first of the Herefordshire landowners to consider cider with the seriousness devoted to wine across the Channel and would command as good a price for his cider as the best offerings from the Rhine. When he was Ambassador in Venice he commissioned the Scudamore flute – a beautiful glass now in the British Museum – to bear testimony to the quality of his orchards. More than a century later Thomas Andrew Knight, President of the Royal Horticultural Society, and the father of modern scientific pomology produced in 1811 his *Pomona Herefordiensis*, the first catalogue *raisonné* of cider and pear varieties. However, after the victory at Waterloo, the subsequent peace restored the import of wine and cider became increasingly the drink of the farm labourer. It was only after phylloxera devastated French vineyards that the French government gave new impetus to the study of cider.

It was against this background that my great-grandfather wrote 'The Orchard and its Products, Cider and Perry' in volume one of the *Herefordshire Pomona* which developed and extended the work of Thomas Andrew Knight. It was not surprising therefore that his younger son who was deprived of a formal education by severe asthma should take advantage of his father's work and start to make cider from the Glebe orchard. He worked hard and was good at teaching himself. He learnt French which was crucial in understanding both how the French made champagne and how Pasteur was enlarging the knowledge of fermentation. He knew enough German to learn valuable lessons from Apollinaris in how to bottle carbonated products and from East Prussia how to run a sugar beet mill which enabled him greatly to improve the reception and crushing of apples.

The first recognition of the quality of the fledgling enterprise's products came at the Paris Exhibition of 1888 where a gold medal was awarded for Champagne Perry and a silver gilt for Sparkling Cider. The Royal Warrant was granted in 1911 and throughout the First World War Bulmer's Champagne Cider was the only alcohol served in the Royal Palaces.

Businesses fail for many reasons but one of the most common is shortage of capital. My grandfather received financial support from his father, his father-in-law and from friends of whom the most important were introduced by his elder brother, Fred, from his Cambridge days. Jammie Withers who went on to found the famous law firm did all their legal work for nothing.

It cannot have been easy for my great uncle, Fred, to throw in his lot with his younger brother. He was offered the post of tutor to the King of Siam which it was not surprising that he rejected given his radical views. His circle of friends included Bertrand Russell and the Trevelyan brothers, Roger Fry and C.R. Ashbee and Robbie Ross, the faithful companion of Oscar Wilde. The contrast between the academic world and that of an extremely primitive factory floor could not have been more stark. In addition the stigma attached to going into trade, which it is hard for us to understand today, was neatly summarised in my great uncle's diary where he reported that when he attended the Royal Agricultural Show in Windsor Great Park to promote Bulmer's Cider three passers-by with whom he had been at college, seeing what he was doing cut him dead. 'One of them subsequently became a bishop,' he observed laconically. In my day as a Worcestershire MP the then Bishop (of Worcester) was known as Royal Robin and credited with the observation, 'The Queen and I do so hate name-droppers'.

Fred's anti-clerical views were a source of great concern to his parents but did not prevent him from having a good relationship with John Percival, the Bishop of Hereford, who Roy Jenkins records in his biography of Asquith, writing to the Prime Minister to enquire, 'Whether after seventeen years in this Tory hole he might be considered for York.' Fred's radical views attracted the attention of both the Labour and Liberal parties each of which wanted him to stand in their interest as MP for Hereford. His commitment to his brother was such that he settled for local government where he set out to put his ideas into practice. Hereford he described as a slum cathedral town and his concern to provide proper housing for the poor brought him up against the clerical establishment whom he had approached to provide land. He received from the Reverend Dr Innes, of the College of Vicars, the reply, 'Mr Bulmer, the housing of the poor is not a matter that would in the slightest commend itself to the College of Vicars'. However, he had an ally in the Bishop and with the support of good friends a company called Hereford Dwellings was set up and later the Hereford Garden City.

As Chairman of Hereford Co-operative Housing Limited Fred explained to a meeting of the Trades and Labour Council on 22 December 1917 how the building of the Garden City had been organised. The City Council was responsible for planning the site, determining the number of houses to the acre and laying out roads. A committee was formed to enable future tenants if willing to buy shares to have a say in the size and design of the houses. The Garden City was registered as a Friendly Society and paid the co-operative an annual sum in interest and sinking fund so that ultimately it would be freehold.

Fred served on both the County Council and the City Council at different times. His views on a minimum wage and a limit on hours worked did not commend him to either farmers or landowners and when the Earl of Chesterfield recommended him to the Lord Chancellor as a JP nothing happened. When enquiries were made it was asserted that, 'He had been worse reported on than any man in the kingdom.' A Royal Commission was set up under Lord James of Hereford which found the evidence of corrupt practices and malicious reporting overwhelming. Fred was appointed to the City Bench, the County Bench and later to the Lord Chancellor's Advisory Committee where he secured against much local opposition a wider representation, and after 1918 the appointment of women. Not that he thought that the political scene in Hereford improved much. In 1927 he reckoned that there were six criminals on the Council. Their leader, he alleged, had twice deserted from the army during the war and never got as far as France. Nevertheless, he walked in his robes to the War Memorial on Armistice Day. Hereford took this in its stride, 'It would,' was his comment.

While politics and a wide correspondence provided the intellectual challenge that he needed, the affairs and demands of a growing business could not be ignored. He found the skills required of a salesman somewhat demeaning to the point that he replied to a mother seeking such a job for her son that 'to be a commercial traveller requires rare and special gifts and a man may well thank God if he does not possess them.' On being shown into the office of a northern brewer who went on writing at his desk without looking up but eventually demanding, 'Who the hell are you staring at?' Fred replied, 'The rudest bugger I have ever met in my life.' The brewer was so surprised that he changed his reaction immediately and Fred emerged with a decent order. On another occasion he recorded, 'Lord Tollemache's butler has just been in here trying to get a tip in return for an order. The brute got no tip from me and we got no order. It is these things which make business so offensive.'

Sales apart, a great deal of time had to be given to securing the right apples and to enlarging the factory to accommodate the expanding production. At Shrewsbury Fred had met Harold Baldwin and from that beginning there developed a relationship with the Baldwin family which became increasingly important. The Bulmer factory was modelled in part on the Baldwin factory at Wilden. Through Arthur Baldwin was introduced Robert Worth, an engineering genius, who apart from his work for the Bulmers also installed the pumps for the new Hereford City waterworks which are still in good working order. Stanley Baldwin, when he became Chancellor of the Exchequer, abolished the duty on cider as *de minimis* and when Prime Minister prevented a duty being introduced on French cider fruit needed for the English cider industry at the Ottawa Conference on Imperial Preference.

In 1974 I was elected to represent Stanley Baldwin's old constituency in the House of Commons. One of the great pleasures that came with the job was the opportunity to learn more from his daughter Margaret of the key moments of her father's career – the General Strike, and the stress of mass unemployment, the Abdication and the difficulty of getting the country to accept the need for re-armament. Her father's most remembered remark, his description of the press barons as enjoying power without responsibility, the prerogative of the harlot down the years was given him, she told me, by their cousin Rudyard Kipling. What would he have thought of the surrender by the present generation of politicians to the power of the media? Perhaps the operation of a Gresham's Law (bad money drives out good) that would be best described by a latter-day Gibbon recording our own decline and fall.

My grandfather died in 1919 at the age of fifty-two. Cancer brought on by smoking and the ever present anxiety generated by his two elder boys being in the front line were responsible for his early death. He was Chairman of the Hereford Advisory Committee on recruiting and as the euphoria of 1914 gave way to the despair of 1917 he must have carried his own particular cross. Of his employees forty-five out of forty-six eligible males joined up. His eldest son, Geoffrey, came through the terrible summer campaign on the Western Front in 1916, the only officer in his unit to do so and won the Military Cross. His second son, Howard, was twice wounded. Geoffrey transferred to the Royal Flying Corps whose exploits in combat against Von Richthofen's Flying Circus had all the glamour in the public imagination that the Flanders mud had not. He survived but like so many others succumbed to mental breakdown brought on by his experiences in battle and took his own life on the way to his grandfather's funeral.

My grandmother was always reluctant to talk about the war. Of her six children she outlived all but one and it was not surprising that she preferred to live in the present. She had her own particular vocabulary: the fishmonger who had taken one of the salmon delivered to him by my grandfather for himself was 'a knave of the deepest dye.' When my youngest brother became Head of School at Winchester he was always referred to as 'the polished corner of the temple.' She was one of the first to drive a car in Herefordshire and carried on doing so until she was ninety-three. Latterly she burnt out at least one clutch a year as her procedure on turning on the engine was to rev it up to the point where she could hear it – she was quite deaf – and then slam it into gear. This left four bare patches on the gravel which was transferred to the expectant housemaid waiting outside the front door to remove it.

Her house was always full of music. Her niece married Sir Percy Hull, the organist of Hereford Cathedral and the Three Choirs Festival brought the company of Edward Elgar and some of the leading performers of the day. A young family meant parties and dances, tennis and golf. The River Wye was two fields away and my grandfather's favourite relaxation was fishing – something which he passed on. I have always found that it is the ultimate therapy. One is accepted by the natural world: the otter, the dipper, the water rat . . . all the animals and the birds that inhabit the river and the riverbank just get on with their lives as if they believe that you have a similar right to go about your own. Add to this the ever-changing light on the water, the music of the stream, the song of the birds, the electric flash of a passing kingfisher and the satisfaction of placing your fly over a rising fish and you too are hooked.

My father and his brothers all learnt to row at Shrewsbury. A favourite pastime was to take a boat from the Rowing Club up or down stream. Occasionally it was despatched to Hay by road. The thirty-mile passage down stream to Hereford must be one of the most beautiful in England. The best line to take through fast water and where to picnic were long established.

My grandmother conformed to Queen Victoria's formula for the virtuous married woman – *kinder, kirche* and *küche*. Her interests were centred on the family and its business. Her sister-in-law, Sophie, married to Fred, was of German descent and this created problems on the outbreak of war. In addition she had views of her own. She was indignant at the way men treated women. Tess of the D'Urbervilles expressed it well although her more conventional religious beliefs might have drawn the line before 'the President of the Immortals had finished his sport with Tess.'

She and Fred gave money to Newnham, the fledgling college for girls at Cambridge and sent their daughters there. She was an early advocate of birth control. I remember her explaining its virtues to my grandmother after a mutual friend who was Chairman of the Home for Unmarried Mothers had told her supporters that, 'She was pleased to report that they had a better class of girl this year'. She and Fred were keen supporters of the League of Nations. When Lowes Dickinson was staying with them soon after the First World War broke out he drafted a pamphlet which he published under the title 'A League of Nations'. It influenced the thinking of Lord Bryce who in due course converted President Wilson to the idea. The rest is history.

Oscar Wilde's son, Vyvian Holland, was another visitor. He had been sent to work in a solicitor's office in Hereford. His employer clearly regarded him as tainted and would not even introduce him to his own wife. Fred made him welcome. Vivian recorded afterwards:

> Bulmer was extremely unpopular in the neighbourhood for three reasons. First because he was a Liberal and organised political meetings at which he made converts to his own views which was a heinous crime in such a Conservative stronghold as Hereford. Secondly, because he was a successful businessman in an almost exclusively agricultural community. But most of all because when he had been Mayor of Hereford and therefore Chief Magistrate he had inflicted heavy fines and even imprisonment on local worthies who were found to be drunk in charge. Not even the Lord Lieutenant's chauffeur had escaped his attention. This unpopularity had no effect at all on the Bulmers who were a very united family who did not mix much with their neighbours.

Despite his views, Fred found himself more and more criticised as a capitalist. He supported the MacDonald, Baldwin, Samuel National Government and urged his employees to do the same. He told them at the end of a speech on the state of the country:

> There are a few more things I want to say. Since the war I have received numerous offers to buy this business at very big prices. These offers have no attraction for me. I have lived among you and hope to die among you and I am confident that I tell you the truth when I say that my nephews and son take the same view of the matter. You may rely upon it that as long as the work people will stand by the Bulmers, the Bulmers will stand by them. To those who have recently been unemployed and unfortunately may again be unemployed before long I would say, keep up your courage in better times to come. That is all except this, you are entitled to ask yourselves whether you can trust

me and whether I am disinterested. I can only appeal to my record which has been known to some of you for forty-five years. Those who have not been here long I would ask to do me the justice of taking my record from the people who have worked here for years with me and not from the prophets on the street corner.

The workforce probably had a sound grasp of his strengths and weaknesses but did not doubt his humanity. On one occasion an employee who had contracted VD but dared not tell his wife sought his advice. Fred told him to come with him to the clinic, since that way, nobody would know which of them was infected.

Between the First and Second World Wars the business expanded steadily and became the predominant player in the market, the nature of which changed. Developments in bottling technology favoured the growth of brands of bottled cider and draught cider grew rapidly in working men's clubs particularly in South Wales. Distribution relied less on the railways which had done much in earlier times and particularly during the war to define market share. Whiteway had the Southern Railway, Gaymer the London and North Eastern and Bulmers the Great Western and the London and Midland. A system of depots to be supplied by road was established which allied with a large increase in storage capacity enabled a much faster response to customer needs.

Export markets were developed. Two particularly important were the USA and Eire, both of which were to play a significant part in the future of the company. A pectin factory was constructed to process the dried apple peel and to service the needs of jam makers and confectioners. Fry's Turkish Delight, Robertson's Marmalade and Bird's Certo were some of the end users.

Fred came to rely increasingly on his three nephews with whom, as is often the case, he had an easier relationship than with his eldest son. Tragedy struck when Esmond, his second nephew, died prematurely and almost certainly unnecessarily of septicaemia following an operation for the removal of his appendix. The surgeon had returned to London and nobody wished to take responsibility for his patient. By the time he returned it was too late. Both as an MP and as Chairman of a Health Authority I came to learn how difficult it is to get one doctor to give evidence against another when negligence is alleged.

My grandmother and Esmond's newly married wife, Grace, were grief stricken and when I was born a few months later I was named after him.

I have a few memories of my father – of being taken to see the new house that he was building – of being rowed up the river – of learning to ride a bicycle – of tea with my grandmother on Sunday afternoons and of the way in which the world changed for him when Chamberlain announced, 'No such assurance has been received from Herr Hitler and this country is now at war with Germany.' He joined the RAF perhaps influenced by memories of his eldest brother. He was too old to learn to fly and was the Duty Officer on an airfield in Buckinghamshire when he was killed just before D-Day. A bomber returned with its bomb doors locked having come under heavy flak. It overshot the runway and came to rest close to a line of houses. My father got the inhabitants out but the bombs exploded before he could escape. The village of Westcot commemorated his bravery in a new east window in the church and he was mentioned in despatches. My mother was seven months pregnant and my youngest brother was born in July. It was a difficult time. She subsequently remarried but it did not turn out well. The price paid by those left behind by the war is too often the real tragedy of so many family histories.

CHAPTER 2

Joining the Company

I JOINED THE COMPANY in 1959 just after my wedding. It was thought sensible that I gain some outside experience first and I began my training with Whitbread, a company with well-established procedures. I was sent to the Mackeson brewery at Hythe which was small and retained some Dickensian qualities. It was a basic training and I remember cleaning a fermenting vessel with an old hand who never knew whom he was going to meet next. 'I had Able Seaman Smith here the other day,' he told me, 'very nice gentleman'. Able Seaman Smith was in fact Admiral Sir Connolly Abel Smith, Commander of the Royal Yacht. The personnel side of Whitbread was commanded by the Navy but most of the senior management stemmed from the Rifle Brigade or the Greenjackets. They had well defined views of man management which generated good personnel relations. When I was moved to Chiswell Street in the City, the Sports and Social Club was the place where everyone from Colonel Whitbread to a drayman who had just finished his shift could meet for a drink. Like the Lobby of the House of Commons it enabled people to meet easily and naturally. If you wished to talk to somebody about something it was an excellent opportunity. Without good communication there can be no effective intelligence.

Whitbread taught me a lot about running a pub and as modern TV soaps remind us all of human life is there. Beyond that and very important for Bulmers was to understand how the tied house system worked. Whitbread owned most of the pubs in and around Herefordshire through their purchase of the Cheltenham & Hereford brewery and the Stroud brewery. Also acquired was the Gloucester-shire Cider Company which was sold to us. Later, after we went public, Whitbread acquired shares in Bulmer and we became part of the Whitbread umbrella which meant that our products were available throughout the whole Whitbread estate.

After Whitbread I moved to our advertising agents, the London Press Exchange in St Martin's Lane. I was seconded to the Ford and Cadbury accounts and learnt something about the power of the brand. Harold Macmillan had just won the election on the slogan 'You have never had it so good' and consumer confidence was returning to markets that had been suppressed by rationing and the pervading climate of austerity. Above all commercial television was flexing its muscles before carrying everything before it. Our leading brand was Woodpecker which was being vigorously promoted by The Beverly Sisters – 'Wholesome girls for a wholesome product'.

The outstanding success of this period in the drink industry was Babycham and the challenge that this posed to our company was to create a revolution in its affairs.

When I started work at Hereford my day was divided between spending time in each department to learn how it was conducted and increasingly performing the role of PA to my Uncle Howard. He was the Chairman and the day started in his office where the other directors, his cousin, Bertram, who oversaw production, Adam Cochrane, the sales director, and Edward Ball, the technical director, also relations, joined him. Letters in and out were scrutinised and orders discussed; there were no formal meetings and no budgets. The financial outcome of the year, it was contended, was largely determined by the amount of good weather, the quality of the harvest and the level of taxation – all matters it was suggested outside anybody's control. My uncle would then walk round the factory and have tea with the foremen. These men were the backbone of the company, many of whom had been the Dad's Army who had taken the business through the war. Three hundred men had joined the Forces and the ability to improvise against the shortage of all and everything was an important quality. One visitor said to me that he thought that we made more cider than any other engineering company. Twenty years after the war, departments could still ask the engineers to make something for them without the costs being questioned. The most gifted of them when it came to adaptation was Vernon Beach Thomas, son of the great naturalist Sir William, whose advice to subordinates was always expressed in the simplest terms, 'If a motor is too hot to sit on, don't use it.' There were many other characters, one of whom was a Welshman, Arthur Evans, for whom English was a second language in the form that made John Prescott such a challenge to the Hansard writers. The interim shift was always the intimate shift and if the bottling girls were working nights, probably true.

After whatever problems that had come up had been addressed, my uncle would then lunch with his mother. If the Wye was in good order or the mayfly up on the Arrow, he would then go fishing. He disliked London. Visits would be by train and end at the Great Western Hotel, Paddington, for meetings of the National Association of Cider Makers or with customers or senior salesmen. He returned as soon as he could. His major preoccupation when I joined the company was the relationship with the Showerings. The Showering family owned pubs in Shepton Mallet. Francis Showering was a clever man who recognised the attraction for women of a champagne-style product. He was very well aware of Pomagne our sparkling cider, but had the intelligence to realise that it would sell better in a small bottle. His first offerings were defined by our tasting panel who were people brought up in the tradition of gold medals and the champagne process as undrinkable. To the mill girls of Lancashire, all that mattered was that it was sweet and alcoholic and looked like champagne. Keith Showering told me later that their first visit to their advertising agents Masius Wynn Williams nearly ended in disaster.

They were given little encouragement but as they were leaving met Jack Wynn Williams who saw that they were upset and took them up to his office. The end result was a mutually profitable relationship. Showerings spent the money and Wynn Williams came up with the little chamois – Babycham. As a bonus he introduced them to Guy Aldous, one of the leading trademark QCs. Babycham was tank-fermented and based on imported Swiss pear concentrate. That mattered not at all to the girls who were flooding into the bars now made respectable by the upsurge in the brewers' spending on their pubs. The little chamois conveyed reassurance – to drink gin invited sex, while beer meant too many trips to the lavatory and an expanding waist line. I believe that had my father lived he would have understood all this and, if he had, the history of both companies might have been very different.

Hereford woke up too late and found itself in an expensive trademark battle in the courts which it lost. Showerings were represented by Sir Hartley Shawcross and Bulmers by Sir Lionel Heald who argued unsuccessfully that there was no case to answer.

My uncle was an essentially peaceable man and conversations were held with the Showering family as to what method of co-operation might make sense to both sides including a merger and public flotation. He and Francis Showering had a mutual respect for each other. Francis's relationship with Bertram was closer to mutual loathing.

Keith Showering told me that when apples were in short supply after the war, they had found a small parcel in the Channel Isles. As they could not afford to buy them all they had asked Bertram whether he would take the rest. He bought them all and offered nothing back. As Keith put it, 'We could trust Mr Howard but not Mr Bertram.'

Bertram was determined to pursue the trademark battle through the Irish courts. Under Irish law, Irishmen had to have the controlling shareholding and our Irish company was in the hands of his Irish friend Tom Jackson. This action gravely prejudiced any chance of a successful negotiation with the Showerings. This did not matter to Bertram who was not interested in an accommodation but greatly concerned my uncle since the Showerings now had the resource to increase their presence in the cider industry by purchase and by price cutting. They bought Coates and subsequently Whiteway and Gaymer.

My grandfather and his brother had never kept separate books of account. When Percy was dying, formal arrangements were concluded which left each side of the family with half the shareholding. Fred, before he died, put five per cent of the capital of the company into a trust to benefit the employees. Theoretically, as my uncle was one of the trustees it gave him control of the company. He felt forced to give his cousin an ultimatum. Either he withdrew the action in the Irish courts or he would have to call a shareholders' meeting to vote him off the board. Bertram would not give in and the other directors voted to sell the shares in the Irish company. Jackson bought them but arranged to sell them on to Guinness at a profit. Guinness sold them to Allied Breweries and the company ended up in the hands of the Showerings through their joint venture company the Irish Cider and Perry Company. In due course Showerings were to become part of Allied Breweries and Keith Showering for a time the chairman.

There is a predictable pathology in the rise and fall of family businesses. The creator is usually a gifted character who achieves the initial success, the second generation are the consolidators and the third generation define the outcome – sale, merger, failure or occasionally national champion. Somebody once said that nepotism worked well for the Rothschilds. Some families like the Russells and the Cecils continue to throw up talent in one generation after another but more often the families that prosper are those that recognise their own weakness and take appropriate steps to counter it.

The Bulmer family had reached a critical if not a crisis point. Too many premature deaths had robbed the family of much of its talent. The senior members of the two sides were at loggerheads. There was no structure and no strategy. For the next ten years my concern was to find both.

My uncle was entirely receptive to the proposition that the first step was to obtain good advice and act upon it. Through a friend I had met Sir Anthony Burney, who was a partner in Binder Hamlyn and a very active participant in Courtaulds' defence against a hostile takeover by ICI. They became our auditors and through their consultancy side was to come Peter Prior, the financial director of British Aluminium who became the first non-family managing director and later chairman. Another person who gave us invaluable advice was Andrew Harding, a partner in Macfarlanes, leading family lawyers, who later joined the board. Gradually a network of advisors was created which culminated in a public issue under the auspices of Schroder, Cazenove and Slaughter & May.

There were many challenges along the way. The division between the two sides of the family made it inevitable that the question of sale or flotation had to be addressed. Bertram, as Fred's eldest son, with long experience of the business, claimed to speak for his side of the family but in practice made little effort to give them a proper briefing. His brother, Harold, slept in an iron lung, the victim of polio, and his sisters, for whose interest he was the lead trustee were expected to toe the line. They were not to be given too much money; it would have been passed on to their husbands one of whom would spend it on churches and the other on women. This was funny but unfair. Of his twin sisters, Joan was married to Ivor (Bulmer)-Thomas, who after a distinguished Oxford career became a Labour MP and Minister for the Colonies in the Attlee government. He crossed the floor over the nationalisation of steel (a cause once espoused by his father-in-law but from which I believe that he also would have retreated). He never found a winnable Conservative seat and became editor of the *Daily Telegraph*. This did not work out happily and after the chairmanship of the Historic Churches Trust also led to difficulties – this time with the Archbishop – he created his own Friendless Churches Trust.

Bertram's other sister Nancy was married to a bright young man who deserted her after the birth of her second son and subsequently became a High Court judge. His youngest brother, Becket, had been shot by a sniper as he led his unit through light woodland in northern France in July 1944. His widow later married Evan Maude who had been Stafford Cripps' private secretary when he was Chancellor and later Economic Minister in our Embassy in Washington. Clearly, there was a wealth of talent waiting to be tapped, not least in a debate on the merits of remaining a private company or becoming a public one.

When I became MP for Kidderminster it was in succession to Sir Tatton Brinton who headed the successful and long-established company which bore his name. Some years ago the *Financial Times* did a profile of the West Midlands and contrasted our two companies. His son was asked how they had managed to survive for so long as a family business to which he replied, 'Because we are able as a private company to get our shares through the Estate Duty office for a fraction of their true worth.' Never speak to a journalist! The duty which would be payable on the death of my grandmother was an issue that would have to be met but on the opportunities that might be opened up to individuals by going public there was no discussion. Bertram wanted to keep control in his own hands and had unrealistic expectations of the contribution that his children might make. This was later to cause problems with Peter Prior.

One of our Minute Books recorded, 'Dr Durham retired yesterday and we made him a director.' Durham was a distinguished physician whose study of tropical diseases had left his health impaired. He became head of research in 1905 with no obligation to confine his activities to the company. He made a huge contribution to our understanding of yeast cultures and fermentation. He was somewhat eccentric and his use of dynamite instead of the spade to turn over his garden attracted attention.

Neither 'the career open to talents' nor the contribution that might be made by non-executive directors were part of Bertram's thinking.

When my uncle suggested that he should meet Peter Prior with a view to his joining the board as financial director, he offered him a job as office manager. I believe very strongly in the contribution that can be made by appropriate non-executive directors: in family controlled companies they can be crucial in holding the ring between the executive and the dominant shareholders.

After I had become Chairman I remember a lunch with Adrian Cadbury and his Chief Executive, Basil Collins. We discussed the contribution of non-executive directors. Adrian turned to Basil and asked him, 'Who is there on our Board who makes you read a paper that you were going to table one more time because it is going to pass before that pair of eyes?' Basil smiled and replied, 'Nobody today but Peter Carrington used to.'

Our first non-executive director was Sir Humphrey Mynors who had just retired as Deputy Governor of the Bank of England. Head of a long established – not to say the longest established – Herefordshire family, Bertram finally accepted his appointment as part of the family settlement under which the company was taken to the market. Tony Burney and later Andrew Harding kept chipping away at him over the need for change. Bertram would agree something and then return later, as if nothing had happened, to his former position. It was a slow and wearying process. There were some areas of strategic agreement. The need to go public so that the family should not have all its eggs in one basket was resisted but the case for some diversification was not.

The wine trade was picking up and it seemed to make sense to use our sales and distribution to carry a wider range of products. Parrott, Dent & Reuss and Findlater, Mackie Todd were acquired which brought with them the distribution of Cherry Heering, Pol Roger Champagne, Hine Brandy, Louis Latour burgundies, Fonseca Port and the ownership of Dry Fly and Landrost sherries. This represented a high quality if not high volume portfolio. It was agreed that this should be reflected in its management and Giles Shepard, a godson of my uncle's, was recruited from Charringtons to lead it. He later moved on to become in turn manager of the Dorchester, the Savoy group and the Ritz. Pol Roger, who were concerned about too close an association with cider were reassured! Giles had been at Eton and in the Coldstream Guards. Many of the next generation of the family-controlled brewers shared such a background. Bertram who paraded the radical views of his father, found it hard to accept that social contact at the right level could be a very effective method of opening new business for wines and spirits.

Another area of agreement was the need to reduce dependence on French imported cider apple concentrate in a lean harvest. For many years we had provided local farmers with appropriate varieties of cider apple tree at a hugely subsidised price backed up by an advisory service. But if we were going to achieve the acreage necessary to support our growing sales it was clear that we had to become more proactive. The average yield per acre in Herefordshire at that time was around two tons and we believed that it could be ten. We had to prove it. This meant buying land and doing it ourselves. By a combination of purchase and sale and leaseback, cheap loans to growers and agreements to accept the fruit at a price which generated a decent return thousands of acres were planted with bush orchards of the most productive varieties at a much higher density to the acre than standard trees. We became self-supporting.

Thinking back I reflect that the price which we paid for Findlater, Mackie Todd was not much less than the price paid by Charles Clore for the Guys Hospital Estate. Some sixteen thousand acres of Herefordshire — now part of the Duchy of Cornwall — would have been a better investment for the family. The natural growth of the wine trade was suppressed by a Labour Chancellor who increased taxes all too regularly and sometimes twice a year to the point that Schroders argued, when we came to go public, that our balance sheet would look stronger if our wine interests were sold for cash. This happened.

An initiative which was sustained was investment in Australia. My brother, David, went out to get it off the ground and by a combination of organic growth and the purchase of other companies it grew over the years to make a significant contribution.

The pectin business was strengthened. The apple-based competition in the UK had been acquired making us the only supplier of liquid apple pectin in the domestic market. The product range was extended by the introduction of citrus pectin. Lime is the citrus fruit richest in pectin and Roses, a Schweppes subsidiary, provided us with lime peel from the Caribbean and West Africa. This allowed us to build an international market.

The search for lime peel in the Caribbean took me to St Vincent. We hired a small sea-plane which was piloted by a supremely relaxed American. He could not get a response from the Control Tower as we came into land so he buzzed it. This clearly did not create a favourable impression. We put down in a strong cross wind and ended up in a hedge. We left him to cope with the predictable reaction and met up the next day when he was going to take us to the neighbouring island of Bequia. This time we landed on the sea without incident but while we were having lunch we saw that the plane was drifting out into the bay. Once more we left our pilot to sort things out and went to look at a farm which was for sale. It turned out to be Hollywood's conception of paradise. A volcanic valley full of tropical fruit and beautiful birds ending in a perfect horseshoe bay with the ruins of Spanish forts on each point. I failed to persuade my family to buy it. The fear was the shortage of fresh water. What a mistake!

In retrospect, the best decision that we made at that time was to introduce a drier cider under the brand name, Strongbow, to complement the medium sweet, Woodpecker, and to invest continuously in its success. Strongbow was to become the company's most important property and by the turn of the century to have the potential to become a global brand.

CHAPTER 3

Finding a Home

BEFORE I LEFT CAMBRIDGE I started to look for a house in Herefordshire. The one that I wanted was Aramstone, a pretty red brick Queen Anne house overlooking the Wye. It was in very poor order having been neglected during the war, partly I was told because the owner had no son. After his death the trees in the park had been cut down to pay in part the estate duty, and his daughter, who had married a Cornishman, did not want to live there. She was prepared to lease it to me but not to sell it. I was offered a grant by the Historic Buildings Council if I acquired it but before I knew it, it was razed to the ground. She wrote me a very nice letter saying that she was sorry to have demolished the house but she could not face a grandchild saying to her, 'Granny, why did you sell Aramstone?' Also, she had read an article while having her hair done which had said how much better it was to pull a house down and start again if it was in the middle of your estate and did not meet your requirements. Aramstone featured in Roy Strong's famous exhibition in the V&A 'The Destruction of the English Country House', and was a loss to the county.

We settled for a Georgian rectory near the Shropshire/Worcestershire border which had housed a school during the war and was also in a pretty sorry state. It had however, retained its trees – in particular the best example of a cut-leaf beech that I have ever seen. It had a walled garden – the Secret Garden – which we returned to life. Over the next few years we restored the property with the help of the Treasures of Ludlow and David Mlinaric. The Treasures were a delightful family to work with; another branch of the family were the clematis specialists in Tenbury. Their foreman, Alec Northwood, was

I used to think, a descendant of one of that line who had built our great cathedrals. His intelligence was in his eye. I doubt that he had had much formal education but he could look at an architect's drawing and grasp immediately whether it would work. David Mlinaric, who became one of the country's leading interior decorators, was a new experience for him. Aestheticism was not part of his mindset and David was a step too far. I remember him telling one of his painters that 'that minaret' had told him to do some work again which had not passed muster.

Many houses in Herefordshire were pulled down after the war and there was a regular flow of country house sales which represented a huge opportunity for anybody furnishing a house. At Cambridge I had got to know a number of antique dealers and to learn something about values. I remember sitting next to Francis Egerton, the managing director of Mallets in Bond Street, on a flight to New York and discussing a particular Sotheby sale. He asked me why I had never bought anything from him. I replied, 'Because you didn't pass the truth test.'

'What do you mean?' I told him that, when I was at Cambridge, I had seen a very good Queen Anne cockfighting chair in a dealer's shop but it only had three legs. Sometime later I saw it in his window with four. I was assured that they were all genuine. He laughed. 'I deal in fantasy,' was his answer. Fantasy or reality the country house sales of that time were an Aladdin's Cave. Every piece acquired then brings with it for me a memory of a family or an occasion, even today. Alan Clark said of Michael Heseltine dismissively, 'He buys his own furniture.' Those who inherit everything are deprived of so much fun.

I began to develop an eye for what was authentic and what was not. The auction houses, the knowledgeable dealers and the important national and international collections gave me great pleasure. I had once been in a military hospital in the next-door bed to a man who told me that he had been sent to Germany at the end of the war to hunt down Goering's ADC who had been responsible for his art collection. This officer's estate was just the American side of the line and he went down to find out what he could. He was met by a wall of silence but since there was almost no food he knew that in due course somebody would tap him on the shoulder for a pound of butter if he sat long enough in the local tavern. This happened. He was led into the forest and shown what was a shallow grave. The ADC had been shot on the last day of the war on the orders of the Gestapo by his soldier servant. They had been through the Russian front together.

Goering had stolen a great deal from Jewish families but their international connections ensured that not everything was lost. I remember being shown by a Jewish dealer in New York a storeroom which contained an outstanding collection of Meissen porcelain. It would have made even the Elector of Saxony, the great patron of the factory, blink. He also specialised in Renaissance jewellery. He passed me a piece. 'Do you recognise this?' I didn't. 'It is the brooch that Charles V's wife is wearing in the portrait by Velasquez.' He also showed me the mark of Auschwitz on his arm.

I have enjoyed the company of a number of dealers who have been generous with their time and from whom I have learnt a lot. Jeremy and Rupert Maas, Christopher Wood and Robin Kern reflected my enthusiasm for Victorian pictures and the best English furniture. A visit to Agnews brought back memories of Rome and the origins of the Grand Tour.

The search for a house was followed by the search for the right schools for the children. There is no greater lottery than our education system. The intake in your term and how you fit in, the quality of the staff and whether, if you have an aptitude, there is somebody to develop it . . . We were fortunate in having not very far away one of the best prep schools in England. Abberley had been started by the Ashton family with the mission to get their boys into the best public schools, primarily Winchester and Eton. The then headmaster said to me, 'I will tell you, halfway through his time here, where I think your boy should go. Every boy has a talent and it is our job to find it and develop it. That way will come the confidence to face the world.' We had three sons, all of whom went there, enjoyed it and benefited from it. One was dyslexic and I was told 'he is not going to get into the school of your choice. All our intelligence tests are tests of numeracy and this is not fair to him. He is intelligent beyond his exam results but we have no way of making a proper assessment.' Some years later he came to terms with computers and got a PhD from London University.

Malvern was not far away and offered a good choice of schools for both boys and girls. The first girls' school that we visited was St James and I was amused to see a notice in the fifth form common room which read, 'If when walking upon the Malvern Hill you encounter boys, engage them in conversation sensibly, return at once and report to Matron'. How to preserve the innocence of girls then was difficult. To do so today has become near impossible. We settled in due course for Malvern Girls College and Malvern Boys College for the two elder children. This enabled me to pick them both up for the weekend after my surgery on Saturday when I became an MP and ensure that we all had time together.

CHAPTER 4

MP for Kidderminster

AFTER THE COMPANY WENT PUBLIC I became increasingly involved in politics as Chairman of the Hereford Conservative Association. Our MP was David Gibson-Watt, descendant of the inventor of the steam engine and war hero. A farmer and forester he became Shadow Secretary of State for Wales. We were by no means confident of winning the 1970 election nationally but when the night shift at the largest unionised factory in the town did not turn out to vote, it was clear that there would be no upsets in Hereford. The backbone of the Association was female. Dame Peggy Shepherd, who chaired the Party Conference when Lord Hailsham famously rang his bell to signal his bid for the leadership just surrendered by Harold Macmillan, was a power in the land. Her son later became MP for Hereford.

Selection committees usually had a female majority and were inclined to favour men, not always for the obvious reason. I remember one MP telling me that after he won by one vote a rather henpecked man came up to him and said, 'My wife wants to meet you,' – as if it was a Royal Command – 'she thinks you should know that it is because of her vote you will be our MP.' 'Delighted,' he said, 'but why did she vote for me?' 'Nothing to do with you – your wife was wearing sensible shoes.' Clive Bossom, the Member for Leominster, recalled that, when he was shortlisted for Taunton, his strongest opponent was Edward du Cann who arrived looking like a city stockbroker. Clearly he had got it wrong in an agricultural community. Fog came down and the selection was postponed. When they reassembled some days later du Cann was in well-worn tweed and had done a lot of homework with the local paper. He was selected.

25

When Clive retired I was one of a large number of young hopefuls who put their name forward. I did not make the shortlist but learnt a lot from the process. Peter Temple Morris was chosen and the runner up was Nick Budgeon who subsequently was adopted for Enoch Powell's old seat. Temple Morris was later to defect to New Labour, who rewarded him with a seat in the Lords.

A few months later Kidderminster was seeking a successor to Sir Tatton Brinton. This time I did make the shortlist in a not very strong field. The fact that I was local, the constituency boundary ran through my farm and that my wife was decorative counted, I suspect, for more than such powers of persuasion as I possessed, and I was chosen.

The Brinton family had a long and distinguished past in Kidderminster, its industry and its politics. They were very supportive and helped me to understand the constituency much more quickly than I might otherwise have done. I owe them a great deal. The rural area included the Teme Valley – the river flowing from Houseman's 'blue remembered hills', its bank decked with 'the loveliest of trees' – peopled by well-established farmers and the professional classes. It was solid Tory. Only one village failed to deliver: that was because it was on the edge of Worcester and formed part of the estate of an old Grenadier Brigadier who parked a caravan close enough to the polling station to offer advice to his tenants as they went in to vote. Their reaction was not favourable.

I remember talking to him at the village fete on one occasion when the vicar came up. The Brigadier was strong on discipline, the vicar less so. 'Hang 'em and flog 'em, that's what I say Vicar! What do you say?' The vicar looked pained. 'Are you sure you have got things in the right order Brigadier?' And fled. On another occasion he complained to me that the police were no longer interested in catching poachers. I passed on his comments to the chief superintendent at one of our regular meetings. He looked non-committal and we moved on to the next subject. Some time later he said to me,

'I have sorted those poachers'. I looked at him. 'I didn't think that you were going to.' 'Well,' he said, 'I knew who they were and frankly they were a lot less trouble in his woods than on my streets but when they started to exchange fire with the keeper I had to do something. You should know that a lot of my problems stem from the descendants of three gypsy families and certainly most of the cases of grievous bodily harm.'

Kidderminster, Stourport and Bewdley housed the majority of the population that made up the constituency. Labour support was concentrated in the council estates and the trade unions, the Liberal was centred on the college of further education and those wards of local government which they held in council elections. The dominant issue was the power of the trade unions and Ted Heath was to make 'Who Governs Britain?' the issue on which he went to the country in February 1974.

The Association was in very good heart, some fifty branches all active and well led, an excellent agent, Brian Binley, who understood the patch and the press and with enough financial backing to cover all expenses. The Chairman, Trevor Howell, was the finance director of Carpets International, the largest of the manufacturers. The daytime involved a lot of knocking on doors behind which lay every sort of surprise, although neighbours if at home would tell you all and more than you needed to know about next door. I usually had a team of half a dozen moving up a street in front of me. I lost one lady of sheltered background who retired in a state of shock after being invited to step inside by a black man in his underpants. Another lady who, when the door was not answered, had lifted the letterbox to see inside reported looking down the barrels of a gun – it was in fact the muzzle of a Labrador.

On one occasion we entered a street from one end as the Labour candidate, a Welshman of the left-wing tendency, came in at the other end. We paused because the street was very much Labour heartland. The second door knocked on produced a minor explosion.

We moved up to listen and the words which carried down the street were, 'You lot burnt t' bugger down!' It transpired that the man had a cottage in Snowdonia which had been torched by the Welsh Nats. To have a Welshman soliciting his vote was the ultimate provocation.

Canvassing in the rural areas required a different approach: post offices, pubs and school pick-ups in the day and meetings in parish halls in the evening. By today's standards they were very well attended and often lively. The efficiency of the organisation took me through two or three meetings a night and practice improved performance. Peter Walker was my neighbour on the Worcester boundary and in daily contact with Ted Heath. Peter was able and experienced and kept West Midland candidates in touch with events at the centre. The reception on the doorstep suggested that we would hold on to Government but in the last week things started to go wrong. The muddle over how miners' pay was calculated and Campbell Adamson's (Director General of the CBI) call for the repeal of the Industrial Relations Act suggested weakness in the Government's case. Enoch Powell's call for people to vote Labour to secure a referendum on the Common Market created further confusion in the minds of our supporters.

When the results were announced the Government had lost its majority but I was the new MP for Kidderminster. The pleasure of a good majority was somewhat tempered by the fear that the whole process would have to be repeated all too soon and concern for the demands that this would place on the Association which had worked so hard to send me to Westminster.

A new member is in immediate need of two essential supports on his or her arrival. Tatton Brinton said to me, 'I will wish upon you my secretary. She is the spinster daughter of a Colonel of Marines and your wife will lose no sleep over her. My pair, on the other hand, is most unreliable and better avoided.' I duly recruited Daphne Hickson who was the most enormous support throughout my time in the House. She also worked for Jack Page, MP for Harrow, whose unfailing good humour was a light in the lives of so many of us. She helped me to prioritise correspondence and reply promptly. A rapid and relevant answer makes all the difference. She also enabled me to understand the bureaucracy of government departments.

The importance of a reliable pair in a Commons where the Government has no or only a small majority cannot be exaggerated if you do not want to stay up half the night. The first thing that lands on your desk is the Whip which defines the expected votes in the coming week. Three lines under the subject demands your attendance but two lines does not if you have agreed with an MP on the other side not to vote. Charles Morrison told me that although his father had been Chief Whip he had only offered him one piece of advice when he was fighting his by-election. 'There is a chap called Taverne standing in the Lincoln by-election I think he might win – ring him up and ask him if he will pair with you.' Charles told me that he spent the rest of the session regretting his failure to act.

I arranged a pair with Caerwyn Roderick who was Michael Foot's PPS. I was lucky because if he did not want to be away he would feed me another Labour MP who did and I was able to give more time to the constituency.

When I entered the Chamber for the first time, it was to sit on an Opposition bench. There had been a moment when Ted Heath thought that he might stay in Government with the support of Jeremy Thorpe who had been offered the Home Office, but his Liberal colleagues would not support him so Harold Wilson was summoned to the Palace to form a Government.

In my ignorance I did not realise that where I had chosen to sit had been claimed by the Ulster Unionists. Enoch Powell came and sat on one side of me and Ian Paisley on the other. As a place from which to catch the Speaker's eye I could have chosen better! Their oratory was of a very different order. Enoch's sentence construction was almost Germanic and you waited for the verb at the end to understand exactly what he was saying. Even then, when he was explaining monetary policy, it was not always easy to follow. I remember on one occasion when he was taking the Chancellor, Denis Healey, to task he was followed on our side by Geoffrey Ripon with whom he disagreed profoundly over the Common Market. Geoffrey told him, 'The Right Honourable Gentleman has the best mind in the House – until it is made up'.

Ian Paisley, in full rant, took one back some three hundred years to the banks of the Boyne and the battle cries of Ulstermen determined to expel the Scarlet Woman of Rome from their Province. The same tribal rallying calls can be heard today echoing across the football ground whenever Rangers and Celtic fight it out in Glasgow. I came to think how convenient it would be that if Scotland achieved self-government it took Northern Ireland with it.

Michael Foot, the most fluent debater on the Government bench, was prepared to go back even further in time to remind the House of the triumphs of the Long Parliament and the inspiration that he derived from the Levellers – usually in defence of the Trade Unions of which both he and Tony Benn had a view that was romantic and wrong in equal measure.

The Nineteen Twenty-Two Committee meets weekly and is made up of all Conservative MPs, excluding Ministers when the Party is in Government. The first meeting of the new Parliament was an early opportunity to sense the mood of my new colleagues and there were clearly cross-currents that it would take time to understand; differences over Prices and Incomes policy, how to handle the Trade Unions and the Common Market. Ted Heath was sympathetic to a National Government with himself at its head and older members with memories of the wartime coalition were more supportive than younger members who had seen the U-turns over upper Clyde and Prices and Incomes as a surrender to be reversed. Whatever the disagreements, there was a general belief that a fresh election would not be long delayed and that the Party should avoid a damaging post mortem. The message for me was loud and clear.

Spend as much time in the constituency as you can and be as prepared as possible for an early return to the hustings.

The sitting MP enjoys a considerable advantage over the opposition in that he receives so many invitations by right of his position which in turn create all sorts of opportunities to establish relationships and sometimes to get things done which make a real difference to an individual or a community. A new MP has a curiosity value and first impressions are all important.

Holding weekly surgeries in different parts of the constituency allowed me to combine with local councillors and the organisation in a way which worked very well. We got to know each other better and many of those seeking help or advice needed their councillor rather than their MP. Occasionally they were looking for the doctor. I remember one teenage Irish girl who came in and sat down. There was a silence. 'How can I help you?' I enquired. Further silence, she blushed furiously and then it all came out in a rush. 'I've changed me boyfriend – do I have to change me pill?'

One man came in and said to me that I ought to be aware that he intended to murder the Chief Constable. There were all sorts of conditions of men and women out there. You never knew what to expect.

Discussing this with a parliamentary colleague after we had both left the House I asked him if he had ever felt in the presence of real evil. 'Yes', he said, 'once. A woman came to see me to tell me that her son had been abused at Scout Camp. I went to see the man whom she was accusing and was sufficiently concerned to brief the police. They felt that there was nothing that they could do – until too late. He turned out to be Thomas Hamilton, the Dunblane mass murderer.'

The summer passed in a flood of constituency activity and by the time that the election campaign was called on 26 September we were ready for it.

One issue had become dominant for many of our supporters – reform of the rates. The property revaluation in 1973 had led to an inordinate increase for many people and exposed the unfairness of the demand made for instance on a widow living on her own as opposed to a family living in a council house with three or four wage earners. The new Labour Government had unashamedly gerrymandered the rate support grant so that the shire counties, overwhelmingly Conservative, got a very bad deal. The task of formulating a solution to this was given to Margaret Thatcher. It afforded her the political prominence from which in due course she was to bid for and take over the leadership of the Party. In the end this proved to be something of a poisoned chalice. She regarded reform of the rates as unfinished business and her final solution, the Poll Tax did much to undermine her support in her last period of office as Prime Minister.

Ted Heath wanted to abolish the rates and for many it was the most attractive proposal in our manifesto. He also made it plain that he would co-operate with other parties in finding solutions to the nation's problems. It was a mixed message. In the event the Labour Party was returned with a majority of three and the Conservative Party embarked on the post mortem it had sensibly postponed.

CHAPTER 5

House of Commons

I HAD MADE MY MAIDEN SPEECH on the Trade Union and Labour Relations Bill and served on the committee. As an employer I found myself typecast and in the new Parliament Secretary of the Conservative Employment Committee under Jim Prior.

How to respond to the increasing militancy of the trade unions challenged both parties. 'Get your tanks off my lawn,' Harold Wilson was reported to have told Hugh Scanlon, the leader of the Engineers. Both he and Jim Callaghan had refused to support Barbara Castle in her proposals for reform contained in her White Paper, 'In Place of Strife'. Wilson's Government was not prepared to stand up to the unions. The Conservative party was divided between a desire for conciliation and the need to restore some discipline. The UK was increasingly seen as the sick man of Europe as much for its chaotic industrial relations as its fiscal irresponsibility.

Ted Heath had lost the unquestioning support of the parliamentary party and a leadership election was inevitable.

There are moments when individual MPs have a real opportunity to alter the course of events and even that of history. Nigel Lawson ran the campaign for Ted Heath. I was invited to dinner and had the memorable experience of sitting next to the former Prime Minister so that he could solicit my support. He got it in the first ballot because I was sympathetic to a national Government to contain the trade unions and thought that the party needed more time to find the next leader. My vote made no difference.

Margaret Thatcher won on the first vote but without the majority required to avoid the second. She had wanted Keith Joseph to lead the party but after the reaction to his Birmingham speech in which he had been unwise enough to define those who should be encouraged to have children and those who should not, he lost his nerve. The second ballot brought new names into the ring: Willie Whitelaw, Geoffrey Howe, John Peyton and Hugh Fraser. None of them received the support necessary to become leader and Margaret won convincingly. She got my vote. I admired her guts.

At the end of the Parliament I walked into the chamber behind her and Humphrey Atkins, the Chief Whip. He whispered, 'We are one vote short'. In fact, Callaghan was defeated by one vote and the election was called. I had been due to dine at the Stock Exchange that evening and paired with Harold Lever. I was certain that I could run faster than he could but we were both confined to barracks. Had I, for whatever reason, not been there the Government would not have been defeated, a thought which must have crossed the mind of many colleagues.

It is the job of the Whips to understand the voting intentions of the MPs. This is not always easy. A drunken Irishman who had crossed the sea to abstain in person was a particular challenge.

The last time that a Prime Minister had resigned as a result of a vote in the House was in 1940. I remember Jack Profumo telling me that he had voted against the Chamberlain Government and, as he came out of the lobby, the Chief Whip had borne down on him. 'Profumo, you didn't tell me that you were going to vote against the Government, why not?' 'You might have persuaded me not to,' he replied. The Chief Whip never spoke to him again.

When discussing Chamberlain and Munich with Alec Home, his PPS at the time, I asked him what the Prime Minister talked about on the return flight. 'Japan,' was the answer. As a Birmingham manufacturer, he understood how important were Imperial markets in the maintenance and generation of jobs and was well aware of how vulnerable the Eastern empire was to attack. He stressed the need to buy time. How right he was. Singapore was the greatest military humiliation suffered in the Second World War. Appeasement may be justified if the time bought is spent in effective military preparation. Popular unwillingness in Britain to back re-armament made this much more difficult than it should have been. It was too little too late.

It is interesting to contrast the British, French and Russian approach to the appeasement of Hitler. Had the French mobilised when Hitler moved into the Rhineland we know now that the course of history would have been very different. They missed their chance and repented at leisure.

Stalin thought that he could buy off Hitler with the partition of Poland. He miscalculated but was rescued, albeit at great cost, by the Russian winter. Nobody in the German High Command appeared to have asked the question at what temperature does oil freeze and their army ground to a halt at the gates of Moscow.

Ted Heath had discovered that just as in the 1930s the British people had been reluctant to re-arm against the Nazis they were not yet ready to allow a Conservative Government to confront the barons of the trade union movement. The truth finally dawned during the winter of discontent but for the next four years I had to play my part in Jim Prior's team in seeking a better understanding of the problems involved.

The back bench specialist committees were important then. We would invite those who we saw as leading opinion formers to address us and they would accept. Len Murray of the TUC and John Methuen of the CBI, leading journalists in the field of industrial relations, chairmen of major companies, secretaries of important unions and senior academics, all gave us the benefit of their views. Only Moss Evans of the T&G, Jo Gormley of the Miners and Hugh Scanlon of the Engineers refused. The Government introduced a series of bills which increased the power of the unions. A few people thought that it might help to make them more responsible, but most people saw it as a pay off.

A majority of Labour members were sponsored by one trade union or another and this usually meant that when a bill entered committee all attempts to balance new powers with checks on the way that they were exercised were defeated. The Liberals and the Nationalists, when they held the balance of power, bolstered the Government rather than restrained it. The Communists had given up hope of the ballot box as a way into the House of Commons but by fair means and foul they were a considerable influence in many trade unions through their shop stewards.

The shop stewards all too often exercised the real power through mass meetings, ballot rigging and intimidation. They effectively destroyed jobs in the docks, the motor industry and elsewhere. In the winter of discontent they demonstrated their ability and willingness to bring the public sector to a halt even to the point where they sought to decide who should have an operation. Rubbish lay uncollected in the streets and the dead unburied.

The Callaghan Government stayed in office for three years after it lost its overall majority supported by the Liberals who did not want to face the country with the trial of Jeremy Thorpe fresh in people's minds, and the Nationalists who recognised that it would be foolish to surrender the bargaining power which they enjoyed in a hung parliament.

The failure of its prices and incomes policy to control inflation and its reluctance to cut public expenditure led to an economic crisis which required an appeal to the IMF. This forced the Labour left to accept a reduction in public expenditure. Some short-term improvement followed but the Government continued to play to the left.

When the Top Salaries Revue Board recommended an increase in MPs' pay we were told that the unions would not like it and therefore we could have an increase in pension provision and allowances as compensation. Arguably this started the rot which led to the abuse of expenses and when exposed at a later date a damaging loss of respect for MPs.

Denis Healey, a former Communist, raised the top rate of unearned income tax to 98 per cent and introduced the capital transfer tax. Given the high rate of inflation at the time capital taxes could mean a total confiscation of assets on death when capital gains tax was included. This level of taxation was a dagger at the heart of any family business. Healey boasted of taxing the rich until the pips squeaked. The knock-on effect on investment and employment was rejected by people only interested in nationalisation and jobs in a closed shop. Britain was rapidly becoming a basket case.

In my constituency the main employer was the carpet industry which was the first to feel any downturn in the economy and the last to experience the benefit of any recovery. Numbers employed dropped steadily and liquidity became crucial for survival. Many smaller companies supplying components to the motor industry lost the confidence to invest and all business felt that the Government had no understanding of what was required to create success.

Apart from how to live with the trade unions and run the economy the Government was faced with a referendum on the Common Market on membership of which the Labour party was deeply divided. It had been promised as a means to paper over the cracks before the election. The left wanted to come out but Roy Jenkins and other senior Labour figures joined Ted Heath in leading the campaign to stay in. The referendum was supposed to be about renegotiating the terms but this was a charade. In the real debate bringing countries together to ensure that there was never again a major war in Europe was set against fears for our sovereignty and in Churchill's phrase, a desire to preserve the freedom of the open sea. The surrender of our fisheries was a particular concern and the price of the CAP not understood. Industry was broadly in favour and the trade unions against. One farmer's wife told me that 'she didn't much hold with that Common Market but she did think that reincarnation was a good idea'. The life of a politician is spent exploring the mind of the voter. Sometimes it is unfathomable.

The gradual evolution from the concept of Europe as a free trade area to which I and most of my colleagues signed up to that of a super state in the making was part of the French game plan that was not understood. France had sent people of the highest quality to Brussels and largely controlled the agenda. The Germans, still suffering from post-war guilt, were unwilling to challenge them and it was some time before our Civil Service recognised the importance of sending high flyers to Brussels.

Peter Walker told me that much of his time as Minister of Agriculture was spent creating alliances with the smaller nations to rein in the French who originally designed the CAP for their own purposes. They wished to keep the small farmer on the land for fear that he would otherwise swell the ranks of the Communist party on the streets of France. In this they were largely successful but it cost the rest of us a lot of money and did no favours to the Third World.

The referendum was won by those who wanted to stay in by a healthy margin but the divisions within the Labour party became more intense as the cost of the failure to control the trade unions became ever clearer. In due course the right wing led by Roy Jenkins, Shirley Williams, David Owen and William Rogers left the Labour party to set up the Social Democrats. The old left under Michael Foot went on to fight the 1983 election under a manifesto little different from that of the Communist party.

The 1979 election was a good example of a government losing an election rather than an opposition winning. Margaret Thatcher had not convinced her shadow cabinet of the case for root and branch reform of the law governing the trade unions and the need to free the private sector of the shackles of the corporate state. She was not yet mistress in her own house. A convincing majority followed in due course by victory in the Falklands and the defeat of Arthur Scargill enabled her to change the face of Britain.

CHAPTER 6

Home Office

THE 1979 ELECTION CAMPAIGN in Kidderminster was a triumph for the constituency organisation. Labour was in disarray and the Liberals tarnished by their having kept in office for three years a government which had so manifestly failed. I was given a much increased majority and returned to Westminster aware that we had a mountain to climb.

I was invited to join the Home Office team under Willie Whitelaw as PPS to the Ministers of State, Timothy Raison and Leon Brittan. The department had a wide remit embracing law and order, immigration and broadcasting. There was some significant legislation in prospect and some important decisions to be taken. The police were under-strength and the prisons overcrowded. Police pay had been significantly increased but morale was mixed. In London corruption in the Met. was a serious problem.

The Prison Officers Association reflected the depressing face of too much trade unionism, militancy and poor leadership. Probation officer pay had fallen behind that of social workers. Both groups were looking for significant pay increases. Many prisons were still Dickensian and the prison building programme had lagged behind what was necessary for years on end.

A free vote on capital punishment had been promised in our manifesto. How to deal with Irish and Arab terrorism and extradition were high on the agenda. A short, sharp shock had been promised for those young people who made life miserable for others.

Willie Whitelaw had served with distinction in the Scots Guards during the war and brought much insight into the human condition from his experiences. I had seen during my own service with the

Scots Guards how young men recruited from the poorer parts of Glasgow could be given a self-respect which they might otherwise never have achieved. Instead of a life of low level crime and prison, many of them had a future in the police force. As one Home Office mandarin observed gloomily, 'We have to rely on the criminal class to police the criminal class.'

Looking back now it is easy to see how the end of National Service, the decline of community and religious belief, the explosion in drug taking and the relentless attack on standards of decency by the media transformed the behaviour of a rising generation to the dismay of their parents. The world of Dixon of Dock Green was no more and the task of the Home Office much greater.

Margaret Thatcher placed great trust in and reliance on her Home Secretary. 'Everybody needs a Willie'. As a former Chief Whip he had a deep understanding of the mixed motivation of many MPs and a nose for trouble. I used to watch sometimes how he dealt with the awkward squad. If the individual withstood a frontal assault, he would be likely to be asked for a drink and humoured with the proposition that perhaps since he was a bright fellow there must be something that he the Home Secretary needed to understand and could perhaps put right. Peace was usually restored.

As Deputy Prime Minister his wider responsibilities gave him an important role during the Falklands War. I remember going with him to a Scots Guards dinner to celebrate victory. It was a unique occasion. The Archbishop, who had served with the Regiment during the war and won an MC, was in the Chair and the principal speaker was an old friend who had commanded the battalion in its successful assault on Tumbledown. We discussed the changing nature of warfare and how technical competence had now become the key to success. In particular the speed and efficiency with which missile systems had been armed and deployed had determined the outcome.

Technical competence was increasingly the key to management effectiveness within the Civil Service. The speed of change too often outran the ability of those in charge to understand the implications. Most Permanent Secretaries were arts graduates and the importance of IT imperfectly appreciated. Even now the failures within the public sector to deliver systems which achieve what they were designed to do on budget and on time are more the norm rather than the exception and the subject of regular criticism by the Public Accounts Committee.

The internet and the digital revolution lay in the future but decisions were required on the life of the IBA and a further TV channel. Gwynfor Evans, the leader of the Welsh Nationalists, was threatening to immolate himself unless there was a Welsh television station broadcasting in Welsh.

The Home Secretary did not have the time to watch much television and I remember a morning meeting when he came in, sat down and said to Robert Armstrong, his Permanent Secretary, 'There is a programme on television which my wife tells me I must watch . . . at some impossible time . . . in the middle of dinner; do you know what she is talking about?' 'Yes Minister,' was his answer. The wonders of the VCR were explained and the Home Office video set to record the programme. It was the highlight of the week for most of the political class and a classic commentary on our comedy of manners.

The morning meeting usually started with an analysis of the media and a discussion on how best to respond. If it was Home Office questions in the Commons an important part of the work of a PPS was to anticipate difficult questions from Opposition Members and sometimes from our own. The ministerial team had to be prepared; progress on bills had to be reviewed and reports delivered on key issues. The committee stage of bills was taken in the morning.

In the second half of the afternoon after Question Time the backbench committees met and were monitored by the PPS. Findings were usually delivered over a drink before dinner. This was also a general opportunity to put the world to rights and some of

Willie's observations still come to mind. I remember him saying, 'We have to find a new Chairman of the BBC. I think that George Howard will do a good job – he wears those funny shirts which should go down well with those pinkos.' Those pinkos remained in his sights, particularly during the Falklands War, their coverage of which he regarded as unpatriotic.

The Nationality Bill was the first important legislation introduced. Its primary task was to control the influx of people from the Indian subcontinent, but anticipating from where the UK might receive a large number of refugees raised wider issues. Kith and kin from Rhodesia was particularly sensitive within the Conservative party. Large numbers of so-called 'boat people' – Vietnamese fleeing the Vietcong – were being accommodated in Hong Kong, and I went with Tim Raison to visit the camps. Space for the refugees was extremely restricted and answers had to be found.

Tim went on to visit the Golden Triangle from which much of the opium that caused so much distress flowed. The scale of the drug problem to come was not understood. I remember the MP Christopher Mayhew writing a letter to *The Times* in the mid-seventies recounting his experience of taking LSD in New York. He had been taken up a high mountain and seen all the kingdoms of the earth in a moment of time. It was the high-water mark of the tide of permissiveness.

The reaction to the Vietnam War and particularly to conscription on the university campuses of America had led to violent protest. The peace movement was high on drugs and pop music – reflected in the UK by the Beatles. It became fashionable to take cannabis and harder drugs. The breakdown of deference accelerated. The job of the police became more difficult as did that of many parents. Few families were to remain untouched by the scourge of drug abuse.

It was against this background of life in the Home Office that I was asked to become Chairman of my family company in succession to Peter Prior who had reached retirement age. I had remained a member of the Board and had become increasingly aware of the lack of understanding between those in industry and those in politics of what it was reasonable for the one to ask of the other. Contrary to the easy criticism of my political opponents, it was more and more obvious that the Commons needed more people with understanding of the wealth-creating process.

I remember asking Lord Armstrong, a former head of the Civil Service, who he regarded as the best Chancellor during his career. His answer was Heathcoat Amory. He had run a business and asked all the questions that mattered from his practical experience which were not part of the mindset of Civil Servants however gifted.

I had seen at first hand the truth of Arthur Shenfield's remark that the private sector was controlled by Government and the public sector was not controlled by anyone. I would look down the Government benches and ask myself, 'Who amongst them has ever run anything?'

Harold Lever, who had married an extremely rich wife and lived in Eaton Square, was asked by an equally rich friend of his wife's, 'Harold, I do not understand why you are a Socialist.' To which he replied, 'Just be thankful that I am.' Listening to him explaining inflation accounting to Denis Skinner and the Labour left gave one an insight into their Alice in Wonderland world.

I wanted to stay in politics but was aware that I might have only a limited time in the House since the boundaries of my constituency were to be changed and I would lose all the Teme Valley which had given me such a comfortable and overall majority. I also knew that I was the only member of the family who could ensure that the values which we had established were preserved for another generation. I resigned as a PPS and my place was taken by John Major.

CHAPTER 7

Business and Politics

FROM THE TIME THAT it went public, the whole ethos of the company had to change. The family remained the controlling shareholder but now had to be responsive to outside shareholders, the press and the City. Humphrey Mynors commanded universal respect and he ensured the transfer of the Chairmanship from Bertram to Peter Prior. The financial supervision and management of the company was strengthened by the introduction of David Mynors, the financial director of Imperial Tobacco as a non-executive director and Richard Hollis, who had worked closely with Peter Prior in the past as financial director.

I thought it important to be able to demonstrate that it was possible to rise to the top from within the company. Brian Nelson had joined us direct from King's College, Cambridge where he had obtained a first. He was outstandingly capable and would have made an excellent senior Civil Servant. He was able to marshall his case and to present it to the Board in a way which almost always ensured its acceptance, and he had the wisdom to recognise that the non-executive directors represented an important resource to be tapped and not any sort of threat. He also understood the culture of the company and worked hard to preserve the best of it. I was delighted when he was appointed Managing Director.

After the Conservatives lost office in 1974 the relationship with the new Government became increasingly important. Peter Prior had got to know Cledwyn Hughes, the MP for Anglesey and later the Labour leader in the Lords when he was working in British Aluminium. He introduced him to a number of senior Labour figures including Roy Mason who did some consultancy work for the company. Peter's sympathies were on the left of centre but he came to accept in Margaret Thatcher's phrase, 'The truth usually turns out to be Conservative.'

The company had no experience of trade unions. The increasingly militant T&G were refusing to unload our lorries where they operated a close shop unless the drivers had union cards. In the docks, where if there were apples that could quickly go rotten, they had us over a barrel. Peter handled the introduction of trade unions well and established a leadership course at Brathays in the Lake District where a shop steward and a supervisor who were at loggerheads could be put out on the mountainside together and left there until they learnt to co-operate. The training drew heavily on lessons from the army. It worked.

When I was working on the committee stage of the grossly misnamed Employment Protection bill, it was useful to be able to discuss detail and also to debate wider issues. I was asked by Jim Prior to chair a working party on the Bullock Committee report on industrial democracy. Peter could not see our shop stewards adding much value to our boardroom discussions and shared the view of many trade unionists that they would lose their credibility with the shop floor and simply become 'one of them'. Two-tier boards had worked on the Continent where there was only one union to an industry but in the increasing chaos in Britain's industrial relations, where inter-union disputes were a major part of the problem, unlikely to do so. Margaret Thatcher wanted to restore freedom to manage to the private sector and saw the concept of democracy as advanced in the Bullock report as misplaced. Jim Prior wanted to maintain a dialogue with trade union leaders but he and Margaret increasingly begged to differ over what was achievable by negotiation.

Coming from what was often dismissed as a paternalistic background, I was sympathetic to a change in company law which would allow the board of directors to take the interest of employees into account. Margaret saw it as the thin edge of a wedge which could all too easily frustrate the discipline of the market place.

I introduced a private members' bill which required the Chairman of a public company to set out in the annual report how the employee interest was taken into account and this, in due course, became law. Peter Prior set up an employee council and introduced profit sharing. It took some years before union representatives would agree to sit down with non-union employees but it happened in the end. In fact Bulmers was the first company where the T&G agreed to do so.

I was very keen on the promotion of profit sharing which was not popular with Labour ideologues. I remember asking Denis Healey at Treasury Questions whether he would take steps to promote it. His answer was that he would not. My supplementary question was, 'Why not?' Knowing that it was supported by the Liberals who were keeping him in power, he found himself in difficulty.

Employee councils tended to devote a great deal of time to employee issues but also offered the opportunity to involve opinion formers within the company in a greater understanding of the economic process. Few understood that there was no such thing as government money, only their money raised from taxation. When Denis Healey increased the tax on cider by more than the consumer was willing to pay and the company was taken to the edge of technical insolvency, few could understand that this was the price to be paid for the inefficiency of the nationalised industries. How a company could be properly managed when it was not allowed to determine how much it paid its employees, the appropriate dividend or the price of its products was never explained by a government that was in thrall to a trade union movement which sought short-term advantage and defied the country not to rescue it from the consequences of its own irresponsibility. George Brown's national plan showed how far the Communist model was part of the Labour mindset.

Karl Marx observed that the drive to monopoly was the Achilles heel of capitalism. He did not understand that the Kafkaesque nightmare that his system would create could not forever suppress the natural spirit of the individual, but in part he was right.

When Charles Clore bid for Watney's brewery he triggered a revolution in the brewing industry. Brewing companies with their pub estates were essentially property companies with a strong cash flow. Breweries merged in self-defence or were taken over. During the next thirty years some three hundred disappeared. Many of them were a loss to their communities. The tied house system under which a brewer determined what beer was offered in his pubs was extended to virtually all products. Larger brewery companies formed groups in which they co-operated in the promotion and sometimes the acquisition of other drink companies.

Bulmers were particularly challenged when Courage, the owners of the Taunton Cider Company, created a consortium of Bass, Watney, Scottish Brewers and Guinness to promote their cider. Over-night more than half the pubs in Britain were closed to us. One major Midland brewer dropped our share of their cider business which had been built up over many years from eighty per cent to eight per cent in a year. Schweppes found themselves in a similar position through comparable support for Britvic. Their Chairman, Lord Watkinson, had argued when the first monopolies' enquiry into the brewers tie had taken place that the granting of a licence to a brewer conveyed with it a degree of local monopoly, since a brewer usually fiercely contested the granting of a licence to anybody else too close as he saw it, to his own existing licence. It followed that the licence holder had a duty to meet genuine demand for any licence product other than beer, fairly. Too often this did not happen and it became inevitable that the tie would be challenged again by the Monopolies Commission as the power of oligopoly became more obvious. That Bulmers weathered the rough water created by disproportionate tax increases and the creation of the Taunton

consortium was due to the success of Strongbow, particularly keg
Strongbow, in pubs and clubs and the growth of the supermarkets,
which acquired an ever larger share of the rapidly growing off-licence
trade in alcoholic products.

The higher tax on cider made the pectin part of our business more
important but at the same time deprived us of the resource to invest
as we would have wished. Had we been in a position to acquire the
French company Unipectine our pectin company might have
acquired a critical mass in a global market which would have had a
fundamental impact on the future balance of the business.

The confiscatory levels of personal taxation introduced by Denis
Healey threatened the future, indeed the existence, of many family
companies. We had to take such steps as were available to us to
protect the company from the premature death of major shareholders
which meant putting large numbers of shares into trust and taking out
appropriate life insurance.

We had gone public at the same time as Pilkingtons whose
flotation had been marred by strikes aimed at exploiting the
company's vulnerability at a critical moment. Some years later when
Sir Owen Green bid for the company, the unions and their left wing
MP who had regarded the family as the capitalist enemy suddenly
recognised that they were their protector after all.

After I became Chairman I used to stress how keen I was that, as
the family sold shares as it was bound to do for all the obvious
reasons, they should pass into the hands of the employees through the
profit-sharing scheme. The employees found, like the family, they
had priorities that could not be ignored and sold shares in their turn.
Despite these sales what remained, together with the five per cent of
shares held in trust for them, continued to represent a significant
shareholding.

Some companies were seen as offering a job for life and the
breweries were among them. We had a lot of long-service employees
for whom I felt a special responsibility. I knew that as a public

company we could no longer just say 'no' if we received a takeover approach. It happened at regular intervals but I was never faced with a hostile bid. I used to remind employees regularly at the employee AGM, which followed the AGM, that they came to work for the company because it was what they wanted to do. We would do our best to provide appropriate training but sometimes things might not work out and they would be asked to find another job. No company in the competitive world in which we found ourselves could afford to carry passengers. Equally if they were offered a job elsewhere that was attractive to them – good luck. When we first introduced an IBM computer, we asked everybody to take an IBM aptitude test. A handful of people found that they had a skill of which they were quite unaware and their career prospects were transformed.

Peter Prior in an earlier life had been a consultant in Urwick Orr and through his friendship with Cledwyn Hughes occasionally was asked to do work for Government. He had chaired an enquiry into motorway service stations and on his retirement was asked to investigate discipline in the prisons. I am not sure if he knew what he was taking on. He told me that when he went to Princetown under whose gaunt walls on Dartmoor I had passed so much time when my prep school had been evacuated to the Two Bridges Hotel nearby, he asked the chief warder whether *Porridge* (the TV programme) was a fair description of what went on. The chief warder smiled and said, 'Would you like to meet Ronnie Barker?' He was taken to meet an old lag who had been there more often than not since 1935. Peter said to him that, given the time that he had put in at Princetown, he assumed that he must be reasonably satisfied with what went on. The old lag looked doubtful and then said that he had a serious complaint: they had started to introduce the short stay prisoner which was not the class of person he wanted to be associated with.

Peter's enquiry made a large number of recommendations many of which came to rest in the long grass. He was particularly critical to me of the fact that no other Prison Service in the Western world had an amateur at its head. The Home Secretary's Private Secretary, John Chilcot, had just been invited to run the Prison Service as once he might have been asked to go off and govern New South Wales.

Years later when we were staying with Kenneth Baker I asked David Ramsbottom, HM Inspector of Prisons, who was also a guest, what progress had been made. The answer was not enough and Jack Straw, the Home Secretary did not want to see him or to discuss the obvious problems. It was all too difficult. Other senior serving officers had a similar experience with the Chancellor, Gordon Brown. Having been a member of the Cabinet which took the decision to go to war he was nonetheless reluctant to lift his eyes from his books of account and to listen to those who had to conduct operations as to what this might involve in terms of equipment. It is now clear that this cost lives and the families of those who died as a consequence have every reason to believe that this was a high crime and misdemeanour.

CHAPTER 8

Chairman and MP

BACKBENCH MPS WERE NOT expected to work full time in the House of Commons until comparatively recently. The concept of their role in their constituency has also changed dramatically. Duncan Sandys was reported to have told his constituents that he was elected to represent Streatham in Westminster and not Westminster in Streatham and one member of the Rothschild family only appeared once a year between the wars in his constituency where he would present a gold rose bowl at the flower show.

Between 1976 and 1979 when the Labour Government had lost its majority long hours were inevitable. The real weapon of Opposition is time and a crucial part of tactics in defeating an inadequate government is imaginative use of parliamentary procedure. Late night ambushes were arranged to ensure that a handful of members on our side could pin down most of the parliamentary Labour party into the small hours. Sometimes resistance to particularly contentious legislation meant all night sittings. This changed after the election in 1979 and hours became more normal.

I found that I could balance my new responsibilities with my company without too much difficulty. The job of the Chairman of a company is essentially to make sure that a board composed of relevant talent formulates the strategy which meets carefully defined objectives on behalf of shareholders. It is the duty of the Chief Executive to implement the board's instruction. It is the job of the Finance Director and the Company Secretary to ensure that the board has no unpleasant surprises.

The UK had recently passed through a period of inflation which made forward planning a nightmare. In 1976 it reached 25 per cent.

A friend in BP who had been seconded to the Department of Energy told me that he had spent far too much time passing papers backwards and forwards with the Treasury saying, 'You fill in the rate of inflation' and receiving the reply, 'No – you do.'

It was very helpful in contemplating the future economic climate to have some feel of the strength of Margaret Thatcher's determination to restore to companies the ability to conduct their own affairs effectively and to bring public spending under control. All the company's key advisors were in London – bankers, lawyers, advertising agents and most of the largest customers. When working with Jim Prior I had spent a lot of time with the CBI and in opposition Kenneth Baker and John Sacher of Marks & Spencer had set up a group of parliamentarians and industrialists which debated issues of mutual importance on a regular basis. Understanding the needs of the wealth-creating sector was crucial to restoring our economy and I found that there was a very clear fit between my work as an MP and as Chairman of my company.

One of the first things that I wanted to do on taking over the Chair was to secure the shareholding base of the family which had the power to deliver to the Board the protection sometimes necessary for longer term investments to perform. The City was often too short term. Pilkingtons would never have developed float glass successfully without the commitment of the family.

As the burden of taxation and regulation was reduced, confidence began to return. Nevertheless I recognised that many of the next generation would need money for housing and education. They had to be given access to cash if they were not to sell their shares. Andrew Harding, later the senior partner of Macfarlanes, and a member of the Board was the architect of many of the family trusts and suggested the issue of £20 million of preference shares. This was carried through and gave the family breathing space.

There is always a difficult line to draw after family companies become public ones between encouraging members to show a positive interest and raising false expectations of employment. We offered an induction course and relevant introductions when we were in a position to do so. Attendance at the AGM was always welcome and there was an annual lunch in the House of Commons for the senior generation. It was much easier for those who lived in Herefordshire to identify with the company, because its activities were all around them, than for the rest but there was a general commitment to the future success of the company. At the beginning of the eighties, Bulmers began to prosper and in one year was the best performing share on the stock exchange.

Strongbow was the real engine behind the growth of the company but we were an early player in the market for bottled water. Perrier was, like Babycham before it, something of a marketing phenomenon. It appealed to people who were put in a position in which they had to drink something but did not know what. Business lunches were less alcoholic and a lot of women were becoming more health conscious. Perrier was a good story. Lord Rothermere when recovering from a motor accident in France took a liking to the local water and bought the spring which was naturally *pétillant*. The shape of the bottle was inspired by the dumbells with which he used to exercise. The cosmetic industry had demonstrated that price elasticity was almost infinite if a woman thought that a product would make her more desirable, it remained considerable if she thought that it was good for her health particularly when it could be a substitute for alcohol which might not be and even more in the company of a man whom she did not find attractive.

It was hard to believe that a glass of French water could be priced at a pound or more in a restaurant. As Gustave Leven, who had bought Perrier after the war, and made such a success of it remarked to me, 'I have never found anything as profitable as water.' In London our delivery vehicles were to find themselves carrying more water than cider.

At a Board Meeting in a famous London hotel the management

had placed bottles of Perrier down the table. One of my colleagues poured himself out a glass and then choked on the first gulp. It was neat gin. The Manager was summoned for an explanation. 'I'm sorry' he said, 'that was meant for the Arabs!' Demand came from some unexpected places.

CHAPTER 9

Taxation and Diversification

IN JUNE 1983 Margaret Thatcher won her second General Election with an increased majority. The recovery of the Falklands had hugely enhanced her reputation and the contrast with Michael Foot was stark. He was advocating unilateral nuclear disarmament at a time when the power of the Russians looked to many in Europe to be becoming irresistible. Margaret Thatcher held Europe together against Russian nuclear blackmail and was, in partnership with President Reagan, to create the circumstances which led to the dismantling of the Berlin Wall and the break-up of the USSR. If Michael Foot had become Prime Minister in 1983 this might never have happened. He was also advocating the repeal of Conservative trade union reforms, further nationalisation and a return to the high tax and spend approach which had so manifestly failed under the last Labour Government.

My constituency was no longer Kidderminster but Wyre Forest. Without the Teme valley, I knew that I could not expect an overall majority and that the outcome would depend upon how the Labour and Liberal vote divided. Labour fought on a left wing platform led by local trade union activists while the Liberals focused on issues which were essentially those of local government. As I had seen in the House of Commons Liberal MPs had a pick and mix approach which reflected the views of their electorate, more right wing in the south and left wing in the north. Beyond that they were against original sin and wet weather on bank holidays. I was fortunate that my opponent's support divided almost equally giving me a larger majority than I had thought possible.

Returning to the House of Commons I went back to the partners' desk in the Cloisters which I had shared with John Farr, a clubbable man from a brewing family with an interest in shooting. He had retired and I was suddenly aware of his side of the desk being piled high with grocery bags and a strident female talking loudly into a mobile phone. The prospect of sharing a desk for a parliament with Edwina Curry was not a congenial one and representations to the Whip's Office resulted in her being found alternative facilities which I am sure that she too found more acceptable! Her place was taken by Anthony Beaumont Dark who apart from his habit of putting down smoke from his pipe was good company and full of West Midland gossip. He was as fond of the media as I was averse to it. Privacy is the pearl beyond price for any politician who wants to maintain a balanced family life.

The new Government set out to develop further its mission to encourage enterprise and job creation in the private sector, to reduce the role of the state and to reform further the law governing the trade unions.

The Labour party was in disarray. Leadership of the left was assumed – in the eyes of his supporters – by Arthur Scargill, the miners' leader who was bent on regime change. Battle would inevitably be joined but plans were put in place to ensure that the humiliations of the past were not repeated.

Bulmers continued to do well. Its market capitalisation approached £180m (in 1970 it was around £9m) which was two-thirds that of Guinness and more than half that of Scottish & Newcastle. I wanted to expand its international business but needed greater relevant experience on the Board to do so. We were fortunate to recruit as non-executive directors Alistair Mitchell Innes, a managing director of Nabisco with an excellent background before that in Unilever, and Terry Pryce, the chief executive of Dalgetty who had a deep knowledge of Australia, the only market in which we had our own manufacturing base for cider.

I had not appreciated how vigorously certain brewers were lobbying the Government for an increase in cider duty. It was only on the budget day when the blow was about to fall and as I was having lunch at Schroders that I began to understand. Another guest was Ian Prosser of Bass who said to me with a grin, 'Ten pence on cider today'. Bass was a member of the Taunton consortium and its largest customer. When I had said to their Chairman that I thought that the way in which they had switched most of their business from Bulmers to Taunton might be anticompetitive, he told members of the Brewers Society that I had tried to blackmail him. Bass, as a Birmingham and Burton brewer was also sensitive to the fact that their major competitor, Allied Breweries, had ended up in the hands of the Showerings. Cider must be put in its place.

The increase in duty announced in the budget was a disaster for the company. It was far higher than the consumer was prepared to absorb. For the second time in a decade the Treasury had seriously destabilised the business. Our market capitalisation dropped dramatically and we had to shed almost four hundred jobs. Without family control we would have been taken over.

Shortly afterwards at a Downing Street reception Margaret Thatcher asked me what I would like to drink. 'A glass of Perrier,' I replied. She looked irritated. 'You don't understand,' I told her. 'After what you have done to my company the only way that I can presently maintain the jobs of loyal and hard working employees is by selling French water.' 'Come and tell me about it,' she said. She asked me to meet her later in the week in her room in the House of Commons. The case that I made to her was this: the Treasury is full of bright people who have never lived in the real world. They have no understanding of the consequences for jobs in my company of what they have done. The Government wants me to invest and to make a contribution to the balance of payments by building an international business. Here am I a loyal supporter doing all that you ask and you blow me out of the water. Margaret said how sorry she was. Once the Chancellor had sat down it was difficult to do anything about it. She wanted Treasury Civil Servants to obtain outside experience but that for them meant the City where, if they were any good, they were paid vastly more and were then unwilling to return.

I also reminded her that our sponsoring department with the Treasury was the Ministry of Agriculture, a department which the Treasury tended to regard as being below the salt. I now know that Michael Jopling, the Minister, was not consulted and that the Chairman of Bass advised the Treasury.

Before the brewery groups became so big and the beer market switched increasingly to lager (overwhelmingly foreign brands), Herefordshire had been a major producer of hops. Deprived of their income from hops a number or farmers looked to cider fruit to fill the gap. The raw materials required for cider-making were more expensive than for beer, it took ten years for an orchard to break even and juice had to be stored by the manufacturer for many months. We had encouraged large numbers of local farmers to grow cider apples, the market of which might be gravely prejudiced. How much of this was understood by the Treasury?

The investment required in advertising to build a brand was also a subject with which the Treasury did not concern itself. I remember asking Terry Burns when he was the Permanent Secretary whether they had ever done work on the contribution made by brands to the balance of payments. The answer was no.

The tax increases on cider forced the Board to reconsider the balance of the business and me the balance of my life. In essence, this meant that the company had to develop alternative income streams at home and abroad and that I would have to leave the House of Commons.

The only country in which we manufactured cider outside Britain was Australia. Australia had some obvious attractions: it was English speaking, had some understanding of the product range and a favourable climate. Our first Chairman, Neville McDonald came to us through Binder Hamlyn. He was at that time sorting out the mess that was the Crown Agents' property portfolio. I asked him where in Australia he would invest. He replied, 'Only one place – prime Sydney beach front.' He went on to tell me that when a Japanese mini-submarine had got into Sydney harbour during the war everybody wanted to move back up the hill and prices fell. They had recovered but subsequently his judgement was confirmed to be absolutely right as values increased dramatically.

Our longest serving Chief Executive was recruited from GEC. I asked him what life with Arnold Weinstock had taught him. 'Two things,' he replied, 'a budget is a contract and cash is king. After I had produced a good set of figures, I was summoned to see the great man. He went on writing at his desk and after what seemed an age without looking up he said, "Taylor, these figures read well – where is the money?"'

He worked effectively with the succeeding Chairman, David Stewart, who was also Chairman in Australia of Ferranti and Jaguar and we were able to consolidate and build a business which was based on the Strongbow brand but included fruit juices. At one point we considered bidding for the Cascade brewery and hiving off our Australian operation on the Stock Exchange as a separate company.

Australia needed to be managed from Australia. We had small markets in Malaysia and Hong Kong and a toe hold in Japan. Then there was China . . .

I remember that when Ted Heath returned from his last meeting with Mao Tse Tung he told us at the Foreign Affairs Committee that Mao had said to him that he could not understand why the West had such short time horizons. The Japanese were doing a good job ripping off American technology and in due course what they had learnt would be combined with the potential might of China and China would resume its rightful place in the world as number one.

A Japanese banker later told me that he was extending his branch structure along the Chinese coastline and was confident that the natural trading talent of the Chinese which had been demonstrated in Hong Kong was there in abundance. Further, there was a lot more private money than people realised. The Chinese miracle was only a matter of time.

Later still Douglas Myers, the successful New Zealand entrepreneur, who had bought Alan Bond's breweries in Australia, told me how excited he was by the Chinese market, but how depressed by the short-term view of his bankers. He sold out his stake in Lion Nathan to the Japanese. China, for us, remained a long shot.

The USSR is geographically more an Asian than a European country. I was reminded that this was the case by a visit to Prodintorg, the Russian Board of Trade in Moscow. Across the high table in front of which we sat was the full range of ethnic faces from west to east. I went there in the company of a party organized by Roy Thomson to celebrate the first anniversary of the *Sunday Times* colour section in which we had all advertised. It was possible for my company to sell pectin but not cider. That came but much later.

We had been dressed up as a trade delegation and were given an official tour of the city. The first disappointment was that our tickets for the Bolshoi were withdrawn and given to the Lumumba Friendship delegation. Red Army gymnasts and the Palace of Soviet Achievement were the alternative. I wanted to go to the Pushkin to see its outstanding collection of French Impressionists and slipped there with a friend. When we came out we were accosted by some young Russians, one of whom at least spoke good English. He asked us if we were American and could we send some American magazines. We enquired if this might get them into trouble since Mr Kruschev was, as we understood things, unlikely to favour such a request. One of them then said, 'Oh, we don't pay any attention to him – we call him . . .' and he looked at one of his friends for the translation, 'The Bubble. We didn't approve of the invasion of Hungary so we told him so. He came up to our campus and was rude to us and we told him to get lost!' By this time we were not sure if we were being set up or not and beat a retreat. I asked a friend in our Embassy for his view. He told me that things were seldom what they seemed. At the height of the Cuban Missile crisis all that London wanted to know was whether the Russians were still on the street. He went on, 'The police are everywhere and if I want to shake off my tail I invite him to discuss the black market in Russia. He always replies that in the Union of Soviet Socialist Republics there *is* no black market. I then say, "Come and watch me sell my mackintosh." He then disappears.'

The Chairman of Sears Roebuck once said to the President, 'If you want to win the Cold War drop my catalogues across Russia.' Alistair Cooke in one of his excellent *Letters from America* recalled this and suggested that the US missed a golden opportunity when the Berlin Wall came down to increase the feel-good factor among ordinary Russians by ensuring that toothpaste, tights and pop records passed down the railway system. When the Russian market did open up for cider we found it hard going as more product was stolen than reached its destination.

The biggest potential overseas market was the United States. Before prohibition we had sold our Champagne Cider there but when it was rescinded cider was classed as champagne for duty purposes which made its price prohibitive.

We acquired an apple juice company – its brand, Red Cheek, was number three in New York State. It also produced apple sauce. We learnt some important lessons about how to do business in America but found it hard to add value in a competitive market. We also failed to get the duty on cider reduced. We sold the business to Cadbury Schweppes a short time before the Alar scare led to a significant fall in the sale of apple juice. We were lucky in our timing.

Our African business was a legacy of the empire. Nigeria was the biggest market but both Kenya and South Africa were valuable. I remember the Chairman of Holts, the shipping company, commenting in his annual report how fortunate they were to trade in such a stable country as Nigeria just before the civil war broke out.

With this in mind I always reread my statement in our annual report with the thought how important it was not to give hostages to fortune.

One of our directors, Robin Graham, had run a brewery in Nairobi and had first hand knowledge of the importance of politics in getting results in Africa. What came to be known as Lonrho skills were crucial to success. George Bull, who went on to become Chairman of Diageo, told me that when he was running IDV he thought that he had a spirit monopoly in Nairobi but along came an Indian who built a distillery and gave a large block of shares to the President's wife. That was the end of his monopoly.

We sold our business in South Africa to Gilbeys but went back there after the end of apartheid. Australia apart, cider sales overseas were not going to make a significant contribution to the profitability of the company in the short term.

Sales of wine were increasing rapidly in the UK and it was attractive to revisit our opportunities to sell a wider range of products. When Denis Healey was Chancellor and always looking for increased tax revenue the market was hammered relentlessly. He also thought it was morally right. He records in his autobiography a day spent with his local Co-op debating whether they should sell wine in the light of their temperance background. They agreed to compromise: they would sell wine as long as it was not good wine.

Nigel Lawson carried no such inhibitions and wine was certainly understood in the House of Commons to play an important part in the feel-good factor.

The major agency that was secured was that of Domecq. Sherry was in decline in its core market in the British middle class and the task of turning it round was not an easy one. We achieved some early success. The family was important in Spain and when I chaired the Wine and Spirit Trade Benevolent Dinner at Grosvenor House the Spanish Ambassador attended as their guest. Sitting between him and the head of Customs and Excise was a good opportunity to bring home to the latter the contrast between the support which some countries gave to their companies with that which we had received at his hands.

I was offered a famous chateau by a French merchant bank. The accounts were far from encouraging and I said to the banker acting for the family that I thought that it was the hobby of a rich man. He smiled and said, 'Shall we say two rich men!' He added that when the French Government introduced a wealth tax any wine that was *cru classé* was exempt as a work of art. There were benefits which were not reflected in the balance sheet.

I remember asking Pat Gibson how his acquisition of Chateau Latour had worked out. He told me, 'Not as we had hoped at the beginning. What rescued us was being able to re-equip throughout with money from the French Government at 2 per cent.' The Revolution may have stripped most French chateaux of their contents but what really mattered in French culture one way and another would be protected.

France was also important to us as the source of Perrier, sales of which continued to thrive. Our range of non-alcoholic products was extended by the addition of Orangina from Pernod Ricard. We also invested in the promotion of our own apple juices.

The nature of our pectin business changed. Where once it had been exclusively apple based, citrus peel had replaced the apple as the key raw material. We aligned ourselves with one of the world's largest processors of oranges in Brazil and developed a pectin factory there. The first time that I visited the country I was asked whether I would prefer to meet Ronnie Biggs, the Great Train Robber or the King of Brazil (the Bourbon Palma still had a claim.) I replied that I would like to meet Roberto Campos, the former Brazilian Ambassador in London of whom I had a high opinion. I spent an interesting day in Brazilia, where he gave me an overview of the Brazilian economy and introduced me to the President. Lunch with our Ambassador afterwards was revealing in other ways. Brazilia, like

Canberra and Pretoria, is a wholly artificial city centred on government. Its social and cultural attractions are almost nil. He and his wife clearly found it extremely dull. The highlight of his week was a round of golf with the Russian Ambassador for whom the bottle of whisky was all important. He looked forward to retirement. The Foreign Office was not what it once had been.

Apart from assessing the opportunities to lessen the company's dependence on cider, the Board had to think hard about the changing nature of the distribution chain. The growing power of the supermarkets and brewery mergers both created threats and opportunities. How to get your product to market in the most cost effective way was a crucial determinant of profitability. Government remained the largest cost. To pay their extra tax we had to reduce the numbers that we employed. We worked very hard to help those affected to find other jobs and in the end only a handful suffered compulsory redundancy. It was a painful reminder of what Harold Macmillan called 'events'. I never felt that we spent enough time asking the 'what if?' question.

There was a story circulating at the time which depicted a gardener, an architect and a politician having a drink together and debating whose was the oldest profession – there were no women present. The gardener argued that everything began in the Garden of Eden, to which the architect responded that before the garden was created, order had to be formed out of chaos and God was the great architect. The politician enquired who created the chaos? To many in industry this struck a chord.

Some ministers accepted the need to create better understanding between government, civil service and industry. The Americans and the French managed things better. Eventually courses were established under the Cabinet Office to bring potential high flyers in industry and the Civil Service together to broaden each other's understanding of the problems that they each faced. The bottom line was that Government tried to do too much and did it badly. A situation which was to be progressively compounded by the flow of regulations generated from Brussels.

Ignorance of the law is no defence. This maxim was now totally at odds with natural justice. So complex have some areas of the law become that only a highly paid professional can steer through it. The Treasury in particular has nothing to learn from Byzantium.

Somebody once said that any fool can make things more complex but it takes a genius to simplify. Such people are in very short supply as is the lightning conductor of common sense. So much legislation which is inadequately scrutinised in committee does not allow for the exercise of a proper discretion.

The law of the lowest common denominator prevails. Lawyers have a field day. The situation in recent years has got immeasurably worse. The Home Office, once a great department of state, degenerated into a shambles 'unfit for purpose' and was divided up. It had struggled and failed to cope with the scale of immigration and increased claims for asylum. A tidal wave of new offences and a shortage of prison places have overwhelmed the police and probation services and the jury system was for the first time suspended on account of the intimidation of jurors.

Liberties hard won since the time of Magna Carta have begun to appear under threat and the Lord Chief Justice has warned that Europe is driving out English law.

Respect for Parliament and the police has fallen to an all time low.

Chapter 10

National Trust

A FEW MONTHS AFTER I entered the House of Commons I was invited by Lord Antrim to join the executive committee of the National Trust in succession to Sir Marcus Worsley, the retiring Conservative member. The Trust had become the ultimate safety net for the heritage. Anybody who has read James Lees Milne's diaries or John Harris's *No Voice from the Hall* will understand the destruction wrought on Britain's country houses by death and confiscatory taxation in two world wars. Just as the English milord had brought home works of art of the highest quality from Italy in the eighteenth century the American robber baron had been buying up the best from our country houses in the twentieth. The first thing to go when a family got into financial difficulty was typically the object of highest value and the flow of such works of art out of the country was an additional problem.

The Trust had accepted too many houses in earlier times without the funds to support them and sometimes without their important contents. The immediate issue was to find the money to provide a maintenance fund which could support a property in perpetuity. The rate of inflation at the time which was around 25 per cent meant that no sum of money was theoretically sufficient. The Government was near broke and the Treasury resistant to most attempts to ameliorate the problem.

I found myself working with Edward Montagu of English Heritage, Michael Saunders Watson of the Historic Houses Association and Robin Cook, the owner of Athelhampton and the MP in charge of the Palace of Westminster in proposing to ministers a series of measures often of a technical nature to improve the situation. Few of them were accepted. The tide was still running against us. Denis

Healey was contemplating a wealth tax. He was eventually persuaded against it by alarm in the higher Civil Service that the value of their inflation-proof pensions might be assessed, and by the cost of acquiring the Sutherland pictures which included five Titians on loan to the Scottish National Gallery in Edinburgh. Finally, I think, it came to be understood that the cheapest way of preserving the country houses which so many tourists came to Britain to see was by leaving the family in possession. A wealth tax would merely pour more petrol on the flames.

There was one glimmer of hope. Hugh Dalton, Chancellor in the post-war Labour Government, had suggested that a Land Fund, to be financed by the sale of war surplus, be set up as a permanent memorial to those who had given their lives for their country. His estimate was £50 million, a sum which was later reduced to £10 million by Enoch Powell when he was financial secretary. At 1977 prices, £50 million would have represented over £200 million. When it is recalled that foreign visitors generated around £3 billion of income and that our heritage is outstandingly the most important reason for their coming here, it is only too clear how short-sighted was the then approach. Demanding that the owners of great houses maintain their property to a high standard and yet doing so much to deprive them of the funds to do so was yet a further example of the perverse thinking prevalent at the time.

When we returned to office in 1979 there was a determination to stop the rot by reducing the level of taxation and setting up the National Heritage Memorial Fund based on Dalton's original proposal which commanded all party support. Michael Heseltine and Norman St John Stevas introduced a bill to do this and Martin Charteris became the Chairman. Commenting on the first grant to the fund of £3 million pounds he asked rhetorically, 'Will it be enough? No, of course it won't, but if things go well it will be enough to enable us to make a good start.' Things did go well and in one year the Trust was enabled to accept Kedleston, Belton and the Nostell furniture. In 1974 there was a long list of important houses looking for support. When I retired in 1987 there was not a single one. It was a remarkable turnround.

Works of art were a different matter. I used to look round the more important sales held by Sotheby's and Christie's and talk to the major dealers. Prices were rising and for the exceptional the competition was international. The Agnews were particularly well informed about the contents of private collections. I was told that there were thirty-six pictures of pre-eminent importance and around six hundred which should not be allowed to leave the country. Of those thirty-six any one of them would require more than the annual grant-in-aid to the museums and galleries most of which could not afford to preserve and display what they already held. Alternative to purchase was acceptance in lieu of capital tax. The bureaucratic processes involved in the acceptance of works of art in mitigation of capital tax frightened off a significant number of those acting for important estates. The Chatsworth drawings were offered to the nation for a lot less than they fetched at auction. The museums' association in evidence to the select committee reported:

> the National Heritage Memorial Fund has already begun to benefit the museums of this country, but the incidence of capital taxation and defects in the practical administration of existing legislation continues to discourage potential benefactors to our museums. Foreign competition, especially from immensely well endowed institutions in the US and Japan is stronger than ever and the threat to our cultural heritage intense.

Despite these problems much was saved for the nation by gifts and grants from many different quarters. The Michelangelo 'Tondo' for which the Royal Academy launched its own successful appeal was an early example.

The National Trust was the custodian of an outstanding collection of works of art. It provided over a hundred items for the exhibition in Washington, 'Treasure Houses of Britain', which was a great success. One wealthy American woman who had her eye on the Drumlanrig Rembrandt was heard to ask Angus Stirling, the Director General of the Trust, 'Is the Dook rich?' Angus pretended not to hear. Finally he had to reply to the repeated question, 'Madam, I am not sure that I understand you.' 'Say, is he rich – does he build three houses a year?' Angus replied that he believed that His Grace was adequately housed.

Paul Mellon had built up an important collection of English pictures after the war which he gave to Yale. There were always mega-rich Americans anxious to improve their museums among whom Paul Getty and his museum with its annual budget of $25 million for acquisitions stood out. The committee which reviewed the export of works of art was able to secure time for the money to be raised to keep an important work of art in the country and this made a contribution to the safety net as did the National Arts Collection Fund.

Apart from houses, their contents and taxation, the activities of government touched the Trust in many different ways. As a large landowner bypasses through their property were a regular issue and as a large scale farmer and forester proposals under the CAP of significance. Job creation schemes under the Manpower Services Commission enabled the Trust to offer work and training to a lot of young people and the Trust got some valuable work done which it might not otherwise have attempted. Sensitive issues included the culling of seals, nude bathing and the response to New Age travellers who were prone to leave a trail of filth behind them. I was kept busy.

When we returned to office it was useful to be able to arrange meetings between senior members of the Trust and ministers to explore points of mutual interest. Another clearing house was the Heritage Committee of the British Tourist Authority which brought together the leaders of all the heritage bodies. Given the importance of tourism and the revenue that it generated it was perhaps the most persuasive background from which to seek more sympathetic treatment from the Treasury. Peter Rees, the Chief Secretary, himself a tax QC, had an exceptional understanding of the detailed issues which was unusual in a minister and he always tried to be helpful.

The executive of the Trust comprised people with an outstanding knowledge of heritage issues united in a common purpose to defend as far as possible what was at risk and to lay the foundations for a more secure future. There was a shared vision and sense of values. I only remember one debate where we agreed to differ. Lord Birkenhead had been commissioned by Mrs Bainbridge, Rudyard Kipling's daughter, to write a biography of her father. She was not happy with it and he was paid off. She left her property which included Wimpole Hall and the Kipling manuscripts to the Trust. After her death he requested the Trust's permission to publish. The Duke of Grafton and John Smith, the Deputy Chairman, argued that the Trust must respect the wishes of benefactors even if they were perverse. John Betjeman and John Julius Norwich argued that a serious biography should not be suppressed; it was an oranges and lemons debate. Recognising this nobody else spoke. There was a short silence and then Lord Gibson turned to Lord Birkenhead and said, 'Publish and be damned.'

CHAPTER 11

Living with Violence

THROUGHOUT MY TIME in the House of Commons violence was never far away. Airey Neave was murdered in the Commons car park and the IRA came close to blowing up the Prime Minister in Brighton's Grand Hotel. Our morning routine of checking the car for a bomb was sadly forgotten by Ian Gow who paid the ultimate price. As one atrocity followed another, the Government looked for support from Dublin and Washington. Dublin was consistently evasive, 'Terminally unreliable' in Margaret Thatcher's phrase and Washington had its eye on the Irish lobby led by the Kennedys. Joe Kennedy, when he was Ambassador in London before the war, was actively hostile and the Irish Government sent the German Government a letter of condolence after the death of Hitler. Harold Macmillan's family connections through the Devonshires led to a better understanding with President Kennedy much reinforced by Kruschev's threat to the US during the Cuba crisis. Some forty million Americans claimed Irish ancestry and the IRA were able to exploit romanticism and ignorance in their pursuit of funds. Ted Kennedy was seen as a patron of Irish republicanism.

The Catholic Church no doubt much provoked by the rhetoric of Ian Paisley and the actions of some of his supporters gave a general blessing to freedom fighters. Just as they had been unwilling to condemn Hitler and the evils of his regime outright they found it difficult to denounce the IRA. Hunger strikes were in the Catholic tradition of martyrdom but the murder of innocent women and children and the nail-bombing of horses could not be defended. A truth that they were unwilling to confront was that a majority of those responsible for atrocities were Marxist/Leninist, more

71

comfortable with the Red Brigade than the Catholic Church. They exerted control of Catholic communities by crude intimidation in the obvious tradition of the Mafia which they so closely resembled.

A friend who was a senior officer in NATO told me that he took his American opposite number to Belfast at a time of daily bombings and invited him to reflect on why British troops were in Northern Ireland rather than in Germany facing the Russians. Irish terrorism was financed by Irish Americans – the American could not or would not get his mind round the connection.

Both the US and Irish courts continued to frustrate extradition. Had the Irish and American governments been prepared to hunt down the IRA many lives would have been saved. The Americans were quick to react when they themselves were the victims of terrorism. Margaret Thatcher was heavily criticised by sections of the press for allowing American planes to use a British aerodrome from which to bomb Colonel Gaddafi, a godfather to many terrorists. A London police-woman, Yvonne Fletcher, had been shot from the window of the Libyan Embassy in St James's square and Gadaffi sent money to Arthur Scargill and arms to the IRA. Margaret Thatcher owed him no favours.

Just as the IRA was bent on regime change so was Arthur Scargill. The miners had triumphed over Ted Heath and secured much of what they wanted from the Labour Government. Arthur Scargill had seen violence victorious and was only too prepared to resort to it again. The Government had to resist him. Peter Walker at the Department of Energy and Norman Tebbit at Employment prepared the defences. Peter built up coal stocks at the power stations and Norman developed a step-by-step approach to the reform of the law governing trade unions.

One way to break the stranglehold of the left in some unions was to legislate for a secret ballot before a strike and a cooling off period; beyond that to restrict immunity in secondary picketing to those immediately connected with a dispute and to enable those who were not to sue the union for damages. These changes were enacted.

Fortunately for the Government Scargill made a number of critical mistakes: calling the strike at the beginning of the summer, not keeping the Nottinghamshire miners on side and then sending Yorkshire miners to intimidate their families and constantly refusing a ballot of all members. Neil Kinnock, the new Labour leader, was left floundering as he could not bring himself to demand a ballot or to denounce intimidation.

After Scargill was defeated the print unions also resorted to violence in their battle with Rupert Murdoch. Scargill had demanded a job for life for miners and no pit closures until the pit was exhausted. The print unions were not prepared to accept new technology and wished to maintain old and often corrupt practices. Britain had no chance of economic recovery if such forces prevailed. They were forced to back down.

Strike ballots, the sale of council houses and sustaining our nuclear capabilities were all policies opposed by the Labour party but popular with many of their supporters. Although it would take time for the Government's measures to create jobs in the private sector to work through, particularly when North Sea oil kept the pound at a level which was too high for our exporters, the tide was turning and the foundations laid for another election victory in 1987.

The nationalised industries were a constant burden on the exchequer. Deprived of the discipline of the market place and subject to erratic political interference, transferring them to the private sector had obvious benefits, not least among them that employees could become shareholders. Freight Consortium, Cable and Wireless, Associated British Ports, Brit Oil and British Rail Hotels were early successes to be followed later by the more challenging BT, British Airways and British Leyland. A process was set in train which was to be copied round the world and which made clear the merits of capitalism over socialism.

Alongside this the Howe/Lawson budgets regularly transferred their funds back to the tax payer and companies in the belief that they could spend their own money more effectively than the state. Between 1980 and 1988 Britain moved from the bottom of the economic league of economic growth to the top. Only Japan put in a stronger performance. More than three million jobs were created in the private sector. It took a lot longer to turn around those parts of the country which had for so long been dependent on their Victorian inheritance. They were uniformly Socialist and suffered from a dependency mindset. I talked to one miner who went down the mine at fourteen and subsequently left to start up his own business through which he made a great fortune. 'You would not understand,' he said, 'but once I became self-employed I was no longer one of us.'

Our education system was too often in the hands of people with a Socialist agenda. Private enterprise meant private profit and was therefore not acceptable. The Irish turned round poor rural communities in a generation by ensuring that there was a computer in every school. Computer literacy meant employment and was the instrument by which much inward investment was attracted. German technical schools were another model which might have transformed the lives of the potentially skilled but unacademic. Labour orthodoxy demanded the universal comprehensive which too often failed its community. It was virtually impossible to remove an inadequate teacher and standards of literacy were so bad in some places that it amounted to a betrayal of trust. Nearly half those leaving LEA schools had no qualification and half of them could not read an elementary safety notice. Labour politicians promoted dependence. The council house, the job in a closed shop and a benefit culture were the key to power in the constituency.

With higher standards of living developing, more and more people outside the Labour heartlands recognised that the Labour party was about the division of wealth and the Conservative party its generation. People whose parents would have described themselves as working class now saw themselves quite differently. Margaret Thatcher and Norman Tebbit, now the Party Chairman, could make a credible appeal to 'our people' who were enjoying their cars, their televisions, their well equipped houses and foreign travel and receive their support.

CHAPTER 12

The Thatcher Achievement

Leaving the house of commons stirred mixed emotions in me. It had been a huge privilege to be there and between 1974 and 1987. I had seen Britain transformed from the sick man of Europe to a country which had recovered its self-confidence but was not wholly at peace with itself. The Thatcher reforms would need time to bed down and our future relationship with Europe was unresolved. The House of Commons was likely to become a more fractious place as power passed to Brussels. The Conservative party was changing as those for whom the war had been their seminal experience gave way to a new generation. The military virtues of loyalty, stiff upper lip and steadiness under fire could no longer be counted upon. Willie Whitelaw remarked to me of one colleague, 'I would not share a trench with that gentleman.' It was a feeling that I understood. The Archers, Aitkens, Mellors . . . what were the values that these people represented?

The fall of the Berlin Wall and the final exposure of the Communist regime had left Marxism totally discredited. Vasily Grossman in *Life and Fate* gives a brilliant description of how Russian and German rule under Stalin and Hitler were mirrors of each other in their contempt for human life and ruthless pursuit of power. All those left wing academics who had extolled the virtues of the Soviet system were hard pushed to find excuses. One answer was to concentrate on the Nazi record and hope thereby to deflect attention. The left retained a disproportionate influence in our schools and universities. A favourite target was the British Empire; the teaching of history was highly selective. *Civis Romanus sum, Civis Brittanicus sum* – contrast and compare? Apart from the fact that the teaching of

Latin was also disappearing to the point of invisibility the commanding achievements of the British past were played down, imperialism lambasted, history neglected.

The BBC mirrored their dislike of Margaret Thatcher in their approach to privatisation and their hostility to business. Competition and accountability were uncomfortable concepts. The success of commercial television on the one hand and the exposure of some of the old Spanish practices within the BBC on the other made it vulnerable. Some dons were not noticeably productive. Oxford was appalled at the Thatcher approach and denied her a doctorate. Noel Annan, the Provost of my old Cambridge College, described the contempt of the chattering classes in his book, *Our Age*.

To confront the closed shop and organised labour was understandable but to expect the mandarins and those who considered themselves to be the true elite to submit to the discipline of the market and the needs of the taxpayer where their own interests were concerned was unacceptable. Who was qualified to hold them to account? Not the grocer's daughter. She was not one of us.

Within her own ranks there was criticism. To Norman St John Stevas, after he lost his job in the Cabinet, she was no longer the Blessed Margaret but Attila the Hen. Other disappointed people who did not share Alan Clarke's sexual fantasies were becoming more vocal. Internationally she received high marks from the Americans but her measured approach to the problems of South Africa made for a bumpy ride with much of the Commonwealth. She disliked being lectured by the heads of those states whom she regarded as terminally corrupt and incompetent. Her unwillingness to be pressured did not make the job of the Queen as Head of the Commonwealth any easier. Similarly a determination to retain Britain's sovereignty made negotiations with Brussels and those working for a common currency and federal Europe almost invariably tense. Her relationship with Nigel Lawson, her Chancellor, and Geoffrey Howe, her Foreign Secretary, deteriorated.

When Michael Heseltine threw his tantrum over Westland and made an open challenge to her authority there was for the first time in the parliamentary party a feeling that she might be at risk. Leon Brittan was sacrificed.

Her tendency to interrupt her colleagues did not endear her. David Howell and Christopher Mallaby were both Cambridge friends. David, when Energy Secretary, found it difficult to stand his ground and when Christopher asked me to lunch to discuss his first meeting with her to brief her before a visit to Moscow I warned him to expect interruptions and advised him to ask her to hear him out. He did so, won her respect and went on to become our Ambassador, first in Bonn and then in Paris.

Apart from her predictable critics on the other side I recall a conversation with Tam Dalyell on why so many senior Labour politicians who had been opposed to devolution in Scotland had changed their mind. He smiled. 'That bloody woman,' he said. I asked him if the shadow of John Knox was that long. The first time I had attended a service in a West Highland kirk the address had as its theme, 'And woman was more wicked than the serpent.' Some poor girl had got into trouble and in no way could it be the man's fault. He laughed and told me that the bottom line was that the challenge to stand on your own feet was too direct. Scots were afraid of losing their favourable treatment under the Barnet formula and despite the fact that Adam Smith was a Scot most Scots preferred dependence to the free market.

Whatever criticisms might be levelled at her fairly or unfairly, I believe that she and Winston Churchill will be judged by history to be the greatest Prime Ministers of the twentieth century. He rallied Britain against the enemy without and she rallied Britain against the enemy within, completing with President Reagan the business left unfinished by their predecessors. Fascism and Communism can be seen as the political aberrations of their time and Britain did not succumb to either. That made me proud to call myself a Conservative.

CHAPTER 13

Leaving the Commons

A<small>N MP IS ELECTED</small> to serve his constituents. Every constituency is to a greater or lesser extent a microcosm of the nation. Kidderminster reflected some obvious trends. Manufacturing industry continued to shed jobs and the carpet industry was no exception as improved technology reduced the size of the workforce. The car industry particularly at Longbridge had written the longest suicide note in history through the prolonged failure of unions and management to act in their common interest. Fewer people were employed. Small business became more important.

Local government expanded. Ken Livingstone's rainbow coalition of those who consumed services provided by the GLC raised business rates which could not be met. Small business was bombed out and he had to be challenged. Liberal pavement politics were based on petitions and knocking on doors to promote a demand for a bus shelter, a street crossing, a swimming pool . . . anything that would gain support and this drove up the rates. Increases were always blamed on central government. Businessmen could seldom afford the time to become councillors and so bureaucracy and special pleading increasingly suppressed good housekeeping.

The rates were originally a property tax linked to the provision of services to houses which householders could easily understand. Once education was included the situation became much more complicated and local politics more political. Looking back over my time I suspect that history will judge the closure of grammar schools the most serious mistake.

I remember discussing with Peter Walker where the focus of loyalty lay in a community. He thought in the beer and the football.

In Kidderminster it was in the hospital. So much so that after Labour captured the seat in 1997 and downgraded the services they were thrown out and a local doctor won the election on the platform of saving the hospital. In my time the range of its services was extended and I remember promoting two adjournment debates on the need for proper maternity provision. Too many women in labour were having to be transferred by ambulance to Bromsgrove. A maternity unit was delivered.

Bypasses are often long running issues in the life of an MP. The Bewdley bypass was first mooted in 1935 and finally opened in my last month. Education, health and transport are everyday concerns but occasionally the constituency hit the headlines for some totally unexpected reason. One evening eighty baboons escaped from the safari park located between Kidderminster and Bewdley and were running round the streets. The tabloid press had a field day with shock horror stories – the drunk emerging from the pub and rushing back inside, the old lady putting out her cat and people taking pot shots. I found myself on the committee of a bill to regulate dangerous wild animals. I had no idea what went on in some people's houses: pythons in the cupboard and crocodiles in the bath. Sewers were dangerous places.

Politics is a learning curve. I felt that my time in the House of Commons had taught me many things. I had seen how government is conducted from the inside and some of its strengths and weaknesses. I now understood that the hard currency of politics is knowing the truth behind the spin.

One of an MP's most useful roles is helping constituents through the fog and sometimes the bog of bureaucracy. The tyranny of the bureaucrat can be very real. A well-placed Parliamentary Question can be extremely effective in making things happen fast, particularly if the press becomes interested. Many people in the course of their lives learn at first hand that the law can be an ass. The legal community should offer a substantial prize every year for exposing the most extreme examples and tabling the legal remedy. Those who come out top in the ballot for Private Members' bills would welcome serious proposals and might make a contribution to better government.

Life both in the Commons and in the constituency gave me valuable insights into human nature in all its forms and provided me with memories and friendships which I still treasure. My parliamentary years made me much better prepared for some of the tasks ahead.

CHAPTER 14

Takeover Approaches

THE SHARP FALL in the Bulmer share price triggered a number of takeover approaches, the most credible being from Guinness and Cadbury Schweppes.

Michael Richardson, the partner in Cazenoves, who had taken us public, invited me to dinner. His other guest was Ernest Saunders. Ernest suggested that Strongbow and Guinness were at the extreme ends of the beer spectrum and much easier to promote than the average lager. Guinness had failed with Harp and withdrawn from the Taunton Cider consortium. He believed that with a much increased marketing spend Strongbow would ride the higher duty more easily and make faster progress in the market. He would like to make a bid. I asked him if the Guinness family were aware of his approach. I had been at Cambridge with Benjamin Iveagh, their Chairman, two members of the family, Paul Channon and Mark Lennox Boyd were in the Commons and one of my brothers was married to a direct descendent of the first Lord Iveagh. His answer was unclear but he told me that I must talk to him — he had Benjamin Iveagh's resignation in his pocket. We met again at Scott's restaurant where he arrived late, pulled out his mobile phone and called his advertising agents to say that he had not seen enough cabs with Genius — the current Guinness marketing slogan — written on them on his way to the restaurant and to double up.

It did not take long for me to decide that our values were very different but on one major issue I was in complete agreement: that the brewers' tie seriously restricted our ability to reach our consumers. We went on to co-operate at a later date in our approach to the Monopolies Commission Enquiry into the supply of beer.

Ernest had other companies in his sights. He won a hotly contested battle for Bells Whisky. As I drove past the Gleneagles Hotel which he also acquired there was a large hoarding with the one word, Genius.

The Guinness family had been responsible for a number of initiatives within the company which in Ernest's view too often reflected their private enthusiasms. He gave as an example canal holidays in France. All these would be swept away and the core business reinforced but that too would be streamlined. Edward Guinness told me that when this process was under way their English headquarters at Park Royal resembled what he thought battalion headquarters would have felt like after the battle of the Somme.

The family had the consolation of a rising share price. Ernest went on to bid for the Distillers Company against Argyll and ended up as a guest of Her Majesty. His target was well chosen but his strategy flawed. I asked Anthony Tennant when he became Chairman of Guinness whether he had found green shoots under the dead wood in the Distillers Company. 'No,' he said, 'the organisation was brain dead and there was nothing stirring below the neck'.

Cadbury Schweppes was a very different company. The Cadburys were Quakers with a great tradition of looking after their workforce as anybody who has visited Bournville will understand. They were also teetotal. Schweppes tonic depended upon gin for its place in the market. I remember being in Australia when the merger was announced. Our relationship with the Cadbury company had been based on the pectin which we supplied for their confectionery and they had provided us with facilities in Tasmania. Their Managing Director there said to me, 'I don't know what the logic of this merger may be in Britain, but I can see none here.' I was told that Lord Watkinson, the Chairman of Schweppes was so afraid of a takeover by the Showerings that he set out to persuade the Cadburys that there was one.

The threat now came from the holding being built up in Cadbury Schweppes by an American company, General Cinema, who might combine with a corporate raider to break up the company. I had to take into account that if we became part of Cadbury Schweppes we might find ourselves in a totally different scenario all too soon. The logic of Bulmer as part of Cadbury Schweppes was clearer than that for the original merger of Cadbury with Schweppes. Pectin fitted into the Cadbury side and cider and our drinks portfolio particularly the non-alcoholics into the Schweppes. There was obvious synergy in sales and marketing and in our overseas operations.

I had the greatest respect for Adrian Cadbury who offered me a seat on his Board and I asked our senior non-executive directors to examine the relevant issues and report to our Board. Alistair Mitchell Innes and Terry Pryce met Dominic Cadbury and his financial director for a discussion. Their recommendation was for Bulmers to try to maintain its independence and this was accepted. No hostile bid was mounted.

At a National Trust meeting later I was sitting next to Michael Cadbury who said to me in shock horror terms, 'The Trust has been left a tavern,' as if it were a functioning brothel. The Fleece was a mediaeval hostelry in Cider with Rosie country. No doubt generations of Rosies had forfeited their virginity in the surrounding fields. I often wondered whether the Cadbury family would have preferred to re-privatise and return to their teetotal roots.

Chapter 15

Centenary

B ULMERS CELEBRATED its centenary in 1987. The Prime Minister
attended a lunch in the Savoy after which the health of the
company was proposed eloquently and generously by David Nickson,
the Chairman of Scottish Brewers and President of the CBI. Margaret
Thatcher responded with her usual vigour praising the virtues of hard
work and free enterprise. It was a happy occasion and did much to
erase the negative feelings still held by our top management after the
damage inflicted by the tax increases. The cider market had not
recovered and more than half our turnover now came from
non-alcoholics, wines and spirits and pectin. The tax on cider in
Australia had been doubled but the loss that this inflicted was more
than offset by good results from the new pectin factory in Brazil.

Red Stripe lager from Desnoes & Geddes in Jamaica was added to
our list of Agency products. I had first visited that beautiful island in
the 1960s when it was a demi-paradise of humming birds, hibiscus
and palm-fringed beaches beloved of Ian Fleming and Noel Coward.
It had changed and not for the better. The brewery was in Kingston
which was becoming increasingly violent, high on ganga and Bob
Marley. More than ninety per cent of children were born out of
wedlock, many of them ran wild and the Yardie culture which was
to spread to the streets of Brixton and Birmingham boosted the
murder rate to the point, it was alleged, that there were more people
on death row in Kingston than in the US.

On my last visit, after Desnoes & Geddes had been taken over by
Guinness, a new managing director was transferred from their
company in Nigeria. He told me that after Nigeria where they
executed people on the beach on a Sunday, he was looking for a

better life. In his first week one of the brewery guards had shot an intruder stealing beer and the guard's wife had been carved up in her kitchen the next day. He reflected that the wind of change which had swept away the *pax Brittanica* had left many people without protection and at the mercy of the barbarians.

The highlight of the year was the visit of the Queen and Prince Philip to the company. They arrived by rail. Years earlier we had bought the Brighton Belle which included the Royal Carriage in which to entertain customers and restored the King George VI to pull her. We sold the train to James Sherwood, the great Canadian entrepreneur, hotelier and rail enthusiast but kept King George which eventually went to the rail museum in York. The royal party had had an early start and as they disembarked King George gave vent to the most penetrating whistle of greeting. This was followed by one from the Princess Elizabeth. Although well intended neither engine struck the right note! The Queen and Prince Philip toured the factory. Prince Philip had done so before. He had been impressed by a display of nearly four hundred different varieties of cider apple. There had been a lot of change and he was soon a long way behind asking questions. The household were well used to this and coped admirably. At lunch the Bishop produced his own Grace which I doubt had been cleared with the Head of the Church:

> We thank you O Lord for the apple
> Which the serpent presented to Eve
> And Adam then tucked in his fig leaf
> When from Eden they both had to leave
> The juice of the apple fermented
> As they stood on the banks of the Wye
> We thank thee for Eden's own nectar
> Woodpecker, Medium and Dry.

The Queen was presented with a Pomona which we had commissioned for the centenary in the tradition of the *Pomona Herefordiensis*

(1811) and the 'Herefordshire Pomona' (1870). Beautifully illustrated, they recorded the characteristics of individual varieties of cider apple. The visit went well all round and we received a most appreciative letter from the Palace.

A celebration was held in a huge marquee on the racecourse for all employees and their partners. They were greeted by a pipe band, entertained after dinner by Bob Monkhouse in cabaret and went home under a sensational display of fireworks.

The Centenary was the signal for my cousin Bertram to retire. He had given his life to the company and his last years to creating a museum of cider. His place as a family representative on the Board was taken by his nephew, Roger Cooke, a partner in Cooper & Lybrand. Tom Barnsley also retired. A former Managing Director of Tube Investment, his wide industrial experience had been much appreciated. He was to be followed by Sir Adam Butler, Margaret Thatcher's PPS in opposition, in government one of the longest serving ministers in Northern Ireland. He also served in the DTI. His own family background in Courtaulds, his grandfather's company, gave him a particular insight. His contribution was much valued.

The greatest loss for me was the death of Andrew Harding to whom I had been able to turn for advice for so long. He had played a crucial part in nursing the company through its public issue and on to the point where it had become a significant player in the drinks market. On one occasion when he had been lecturing at Oxford a don had asked him from where his deep and obvious affection for the law had stemmed. 'Love of the law? I hate the law and see my job as keeping people out of it,' Andrew replied. Anyone who has read *Bleak House* will understand the wisdom of his comment.

During our centenary it was announced that the beer industry was to be investigated as a complex monopoly. A process was set in train which was to have fundamental implications for almost everybody in the drink industry. It never crossed my mind at that time that I would live to see Bass and Whitbread go out of brewing.

CHAPTER 16

Poston and Sir William Chambers

I NOW HAD TO COME to terms with my new life. I was about to remarry and we had to find somewhere to live in Herefordshire. I had first met Susan Murray when we were both a lot younger. We had spent a good deal of time together and then lost touch after her marriage broke up. Years later we met again in the House of Commons. We both felt that we had seen the best of London. The city of our youth where you could go where you liked without having to look over your shoulder, park the car or walk the dog without a thought had gone. When I was a serving officer in Wellington Barracks a small house in Chelsea cost £5,000 and a good night out £3. The square where I was living had been bought by an Arab and the house was full of Jews – a proxy Middle East war loomed. Throughout London pockets of immigrants from different countries were expanding and changing the balance of the population. Drugs were fuelling the mugger and the burglar.

We had learnt to live with the IRA but while multiculturalism was the panacea peddled by the BBC and *The Guardian*, for many who had to experience it at close quarters it was far from comfortable. Go to London to grow up, meet people and perhaps make your fortune, but when it came to bringing up children few of our friends would choose London to do so if there was a viable alternative.

Herefordshire is one of the most beautiful counties in England. We found what we were looking for in the Golden Valley. In the lea of the Black Mountains it was the first farmland that the Romans were determined to defend against the Welsh, an assessment shared by the Normans who built Dore Abbey, the great Cistercian church which glowed in our middle view as it picked up the rays of the sun setting in the west. What we were to acquire looked like a derelict farm with nothing to commend it. What lay hidden within it was a casino built by Sir William Chambers with an outstanding view to the east to Garway Hill, traversing the whole line of the Black Mountains to the south and west towards the middle Wye. The eighteenth century plasterwork was frail but not beyond restoration; dry rot was everywhere.

Through David Mlinaric we met Philip Jebb who had restored so many properties for the Landmark Trust. John Smith's achievement in bringing back to life a kaleidoscope of unique features in our landscape is one of the unsung successes of our post-war crusade to defend our heritage. Philip was the most delightful of men, his scholarship worn lightly but always to hand with the inspired solution and the beautiful drawing. He quickly established a partnership with Stephen Treasure whose firm had been such a support to me in the past. For the next eight years we restored what Chambers had designed and then set about related buildings. Philip had an outstanding eye for proportion and using old brick a small walled garden and an orangerie replaced dilapidated cowsheds. The farmhouse and adjacent cottages were also remodelled.

To restore to former glory and to create are some of the higher pleasures of life. Moving from one project to the next gave us continuous stimulus. Palladio is the great inspiration behind the classical facade of Augustan Britain. We spent many happy holidays in the Veneto exploring his legacy. In earlier years I had had a short flirtation with the Villa Valmorana Ai Nani – the villa of the dwarfs, so called after its Tiepolo decoration. Both Gianbattista and Giandomenico had worked there but American bombing had shaken the structure. The family were threatened by the Red Brigade and put the house on the market. The surroundings were no longer beautiful and I went no further. It never crossed my mind to emulate Sebastian Ferranti who so successfully recreated the Villa Capra on his Cheshire estate. I asked him, when Susie and I were staying with him, whether he would have done anything differently if he were starting again. 'Yes,' he said, 'pushed it out a metre all round.' Naomi interjected, 'Yes, and you would have gone bankrupt. The loos are flushing hot water and HRH is expected in half an hour.' Wives can bring us down to earth so quickly.

In Italy it was the Red Brigade, in England the IRA. We had to think about security. Charles Tidbury, a friend who was Chairman of Whitbread, was targeted for apparently no better reason than leading the appeal for the *Mary Rose*, Henry VIII's great battleship. He told of being woken in the middle of the night by the police to be informed that he had company. The IRA gang escaped.

We had the SAS all around us. When the crime protection officer came to visit, Susie said to him, 'If Esmond is away and I hear a man coming down the passage towards me can I shoot him?' The policeman grinned and said, 'Don't miss with the first barrel and put the second barrel into the ceiling to show that you warned him.'

Our biggest concern was the footpath. They are almost impossible to extinguish but sometimes may be varied although this is a time-consuming process. When we were staying with the Home Secretary at Dorneywood a French minister who was also a guest saw people walking through the garden. He enquired who they were. It was explained to him that they were using a public footpath. He looked at me. '*Les Anglais sont fous n'est ce pas?*' A footpath that passed Chequers from which it was theoretically possible to shoot somebody on the terrace was eventually moved

It was a great shock when Philip Jebb told us that he had terminal cancer. His humour and humility and deep Catholic faith enabled him to contemplate the end of his days with the serenity given only to the exceptional. His funeral service taken by his brother, the Prior of Downside, was deeply moving. He always remained for us part of the spirit of Poston.

Beyond the building work lay the park first enclosed in the reign of Elizabeth I for hunting. It too offered a great deal of scope for improvement. We planted trees and thinned the adjacent woodland. Soay sheep and Exmoor ponies replaced the deer and the buzzards wheeled overhead. Our dogs enjoyed their own private world of the fox, the badger and the rabbit and were always demanding the next foray. We loved the place.

CHAPTER 17

Rebalancing the Business

THE END OF THE DECADE brought changes which once more led Bulmers to review its strategy. The Monopolies Commission had found that the Taunton Cider Company was structured in a way which was anti-competitive and the participating brewers would have to withdraw. The break-up of the Soviet Union reduced the world demand for pectin and a cancer scare relating to a trace mineral in Perrier led to the withdrawal of all its product in circulation.

Brian Nelson retired as Chief Executive having taken the company through some very difficult water and achieved some outstanding successes. Had the duty changes been less harsh his contribution would have received wider recognition. He built a talented team around him. He was succeeded by John Rudgard who was running the cider company and had spent most of his career within it. Brian was appointed Chairman of the Home Grown Cereal Authority.

Companies frequently diversify and then return to their core business. This seemed to be the way ahead for us. The opportunities to exploit the changes in the competition in the cider market were obvious. The Board decided to double the marketing spend behind Strongbow even though this meant reducing the company's profits significantly. It was able to do so because the family shareholding gave it protection against an opportunistic takeover bid and the City recognised that it was a credible move.

The water market continued to grow. Perrier was the out and out brand leader but the recall did it great damage. I was sitting next to the head of British Nuclear Fuels at lunch when he said to me, 'I see that you have a little local difficulty – I don't suppose that they could have measured it ten years ago. When they come on heavy with me I tell them that my benchmark is Hiroshima.'

Nuclear safety became a major international issue after the explosion at the Chernobyl power station. The Russians were buying pectin from us which they were making into a paste to counter the effects of radiation. We never understood the science behind their approach but in the free for all that followed the fall of the Communist Party, the purchase of pectin dropped dramatically. Chernobyl remained a constant reminder of the threat posed by so much nuclear activity within the USSR which was past its sell-by date and might go into free fall. Leon Brittan told me years later that at a meeting with the President of the Ukraine he was informed that Chernobyl remained dangerous but still provided too much power which could not be replaced to be closed down. The Ukraine needed help if it was to do without it. The EEC provided it but as so often only a fraction got through to where it was intended to go. The balance of supply and demand in the pectin market shifted and prices fell. In due course we sold out.

Apart from the increased advertising of Strongbow we acquired niche cider companies at home and abroad in expanding our cider interests, and beer increasingly replaced wines and spirits as the base of our agency business. Nestlé acquired Perrier and transferred the agency to Cadbury Schweppes. This meant that our soft drinks business became less viable. The key question for us in the UK was what would happen to the Taunton Cider Company: our futures were inextricably linked and how they played out would determine the direction of the cider market.

A further question which hung in the air was what in practice did the European single market mean for us and was the harmonisation of the duty levels on alcoholic drink across the Community ever going to happen? Norman Lamont had said in a budget speech that he would not allow Brussels to ride roughshod over the English cider industry. We needed to improve our understanding of what might happen.

We bought Stassen, a Belgian cider maker, whose premises were not far from Maastricht. In minutes you could be in four different countries. People there had suffered from living in the cockpit of Europe for centuries and you could almost hear the rumble of the German Panzers churning through the Ardennes. To the Belgians the case for Federal Europe was irresistible. 'Peace in our Time'.

In Westminster it looked rather different. Britain had not been invaded for nearly a thousand years. The success of her democratic traditions and her history as the world's most successful trading nation made it difficult to accept that she should surrender powers to act in her own best interest and to submit to an unaccountable bureaucracy. Northern Europe drank beer, southern Europe drank wine. This distinction sat alongside other important differences: the north was cold, Protestant, hard-working and had a respect for the law; the south was hot, Catholic, enjoyed a siesta and too often seemed to regard the law as being written for other people. They were not natural bedfellows.

In the post-Thatcher period either the battle over ever closer union in Westminster or the introduction of PR had the potential to break the mould of British politics. In my view the BBC too often lacked intellectual rigour in its coverage of the issues, seldom differentiating between the case for the euro and the case for general co-operation in a market short of surrendering sovereignty. Anyone who had doubts about the euro was not a European and likely to be dismissed as a little Englander. The BBC had power apparently without responsibility. It was difficult to challenge in important respects and too often chose who it interviewed to reflect its own agenda. Similarly in its attitude to business, it seemed never to define profit in relation to return on capital employed and it seldom portrayed an entrepreneur or a manager in a favourable light. It played to the gallery secure in its licence fee and comfortable enjoyment thereof. John Birt's description of its inefficiencies if found in the private sector would have been placed firmly in the spotlight.

There were no short answers to Britain's future in Europe. The purchase of Stassen gave us a much improved awareness of the way in which the Brussels bureaucracy functioned. It was essential to understand what was being contemplated well before proposals were tabled if you wanted to influence the course of events. Brussels could make or break a company. It had the power to define or to redefine a product and to take decisions on safety and environmental grounds which could dramatically increase costs. It represented a growing burden on management in many different ways and no sensible company could ignore its activities in defining the threats and opportunities to be taken into account in plotting its future. Having been sandbagged twice by the British Government we had to look to our defences across the Channel.

My understanding of attitudes within the Community was in part based on experiences with the families for whom we acted as agents.

Copenhagen is famous for the Carlsberg brewery. I first went there as the guest of Peter Heering whose cherry brandy we sold. He had handsome offices which he showed me round. He opened the door to the Boardroom and told me, 'This is the Boardroom: I am the Board'. He built one ship a year and used the profits from his liqueurs to pay for the depreciation. The ship was then sold when the market conditions were right. The company who acted for him in Germany was Henkel. Ribbentrop, Hitler's foreign minister, had married Miss Henkel and Ribbentrop was sometimes dismissed as the champagne salesman. Peter introduced me to his son, Adolf, named after his godfather. Adolf spoke perfect English and could have passed as an Englishman. His father was executed after the Nuremberg trials but I was told that the Russians were prepared to spare his life if he would testify that it was the Germans who had murdered the Polish officer class at Katyn. The Ribbentrop/Molotov pact placed the Russians in an impossible position. Their treatment of the Poles deserved to put them in the dock alongside the Nazis.

I was talking to Adolf when a Professor of Law at the university whom I had met earlier, approached. I knew that he was a Jew and that I could not possibly introduce the one to the other; I pretended to have a nosebleed and fled. Afterwards, I explained to Peter Heering what had happened. He told me something of his life in Denmark under German occupation when he had been a prominent member of the underground keeping those most at risk out of the clutches of the Gestapo. He was trying to forget the past but it was so difficult.

Years later we acted for Henkel in England. I remember a telephone call from Adolf to say that he would like to meet some English brewers and suggested that he brought Margaret with him. Margaret was Margaret Goebbels – no relation – who was the sales director of a company acting for some important estates on the Rhine and Mosel whose wine we distributed. I reflected on how some of my brewing friends would react to an invitation to lunch with Ribbentrop and Goebbels. It was a long time before the shadow of the war began to fade. In France the Pol Roger family had suffered at the hands of the Germans but the war had a silver lining. When Winston Churchill came to Paris to celebrate its liberation he met Odette Pol Roger. She was a beautiful woman and he became Pol Roger's most important customer. In his last decade a hundred cases passed through his cellar and when he died a special *cuvée* was dedicated to his memory.

Many Frenchmen did not want to be reminded of the war. In a friend's house in Paris my uncle whose French consisted of a very limited vocabulary from the First World War was introduced to a French Admiral. The Admiral spoke no English, or if he did, would not disclose the fact, and my uncle tried his disastrous French. They were soon totally at cross purposes and I realised that my uncle was trying to talk about the First World War and that the Admiral had been sunk by the British Navy in Toulon Harbour in the Second.

The French were not natural allies of the English or the Germans and I remember having lunch with President Mitterand's interpreter before the Berlin Wall came down. The Elysée was confident that Europe had to revolve around the French landmass, the key task was to restore the hegemony of the French language. France would play both sides against the middle and its grip on the Brussels bureaucracy would ensure that French interests prevailed. It was a very clear steer.

The shadow of a very different war hung over Spain. The Domecq family had been important supporters of Franco. I was asked by a member of the family after lunch whether I would like to see his guns. I anticipated pairs of Purdeys – they had outstanding partridge shooting. In the event I was taken to a stable block which housed arms for a regiment. Spain had its own reasons for supporting Federal Europe.

Portugal was probably the poorest country in the single market and stood to do well out of membership of the Community. Oporto was a time capsule. Dent & Reuss, our wine shipping company, represented Fonseca, which was owned by Taylor Fladgate and Yeatman. On my first visit I was taken to lunch in the Factory House, a period building with Chippendale furniture where the port wine shippers discussed their business. After lunch we went to the cricket ground to watch their team play the Fleet. This now consisted of one destroyer. Dick Yeatman, who owned Taylors, had recently married late in life and I realised when we met that his wife was a little out of sorts. It transpired that Dick had driven her home to her parents' house the night before after dining with friends having forgotten that he had married her. Life went on, sometimes in a pleasant state of amnesia.

The English community was very well integrated with the host nation with which we have enjoyed our longest trading connection. We had never been the colonial power and the relationship was a good one. Soon after our first visit Giles Shepard and I were asked to Lisbon to meet the Duke of Cavadal, Portugal's premier Duke whose father had been exiled by Salazar. He had been told that he could be rehabilitated if he returned and managed his estates. He had been impressed by the success of Mateus Rosé and thought that if the Cadaval arms were put on the label of his house wine we might be prepared to distribute it for him. Bruce Guimaraens whose family had originally owned Fonseca came with us. We drove out of Lisbon with the Duke and his chauffeur, neither of whom appeared to know where the wine for which we were looking was located. The chauffeur kept having to enquire whether this was His Grace's property and eventually we arrived at where we were supposed to be. Bruce sampled the wine. 'Just good enough to be blended into Vermouth in an off year,' he whispered to me. We proceeded no further. When the revolution came I was not surprised to read that the Cadaval estates were the first to be occupied. Portugal after it had recovered its equilibrium was unlikely to vote against ever closer union with the Community.

In Italy we represented Ingham Whitaker, whose main claim to fame was that they had stocked Nelson with Marsala en route for Aboukir Bay, where he had annihilated the French fleet. To my surprise there was a bust of Mussolini and I was told that Il Duce was only otherwise on display in the Opera House where it was felt that the over-decorated ceiling might collapse if it was removed. Sicily was an ardent recipient of Community funds only a fraction of which ever reached the destination for which they had been intended. It was after all the home of the Mafia. Italy had only been unified for just over a century and Federal Europe was an attractive concept to many who despaired of the conduct of Italian politicians.

George Canning famously remarked that he had brought the New World in to redress the balance of the Old. The Foreign Office must have called this to mind when deducing as I had that without the countries of the newly liberated Eastern Europe being brought into the equation the move to ever closer union would be irresistible and the surrender of sovereignty relentless.

After the Labour Government came to power in 1997 I attended a CBI dinner with the Secretary of State for Trade. Adair Turner, the Director General, told us that the Prime Minister did not want to hold a referendum on the euro without the full hearted support of the CBI and suggested that we would want to give it. He went round the table: Chairman of BA, Chairman of BT, Chairman of . . . bloody everything, I thought as they all spoke in favour hoping for something from Downing Street. When it came to my turn I said to Stephen Byers who had just replaced Peter Mandelson, 'You know and I know that the euro is a political decision first, middle and last and unless you are prepared to publish a White Paper setting out the political implications I do not believe that the CBI should be joined in selling a false prospectus.' Stephen Byers said that he was sure that the Prime Minister would see that all the relevant arguments were rehearsed.

I telephoned Michael Brinton to discuss the attitude of the West Midland CBI and we agreed that action should be taken to see that the issues were properly debated. A lot of other people thought the same. The case for the euro would not go unchallenged. It had to be seen as another step on the way to inclusion in Federal Europe, any decision on which should be left to the British people to determine.

CHAPTER 18

The City of London

THE GOODWILL OF THE CITY is important for a company. I tried to read the wind from the inside and how it was changing. I have lived through the death of gentlemanly capitalism. At the time that Humphrey Mynors joined our Board the Governor had only to raise an eyebrow and the questionable activity ceased.

I remember having lunch at Flemings with Charles Nunneley, an old friend. Richard Fleming came in late and apologised. 'I am sorry – I have had the most extraordinary man in my office. I am not sure whether he will be Prime Minister or go to prison'. Few people would have mistaken Robert Maxwell for a gentleman or failed to feel the force of his personality. His was not the world of good manners or respect for any rules that he did not find convenient. Flemings had a hard time with him when they were joined in Pergamon. His later history heaped embarrassments on the Labour Party but before his final disgrace he was still able to wheel out an ailing Harold Wilson to eulogise his achievements. Maxwell and his kind made the introduction of legislation to regulate their activities inevitable. Too often it was closing the stable door after the horse had bolted.

After Big Bang I was asked by Nicholas Goodison to serve on the Stock Exchange Listed Companies Advisory Committee. I accepted because I felt that the family-controlled company was too often caught up in a web of legislation in a way that was not necessarily intended. The attitude to non-executive directors was increasingly to regard them as policemen which was totally at odds with our approach. They were first and foremost part of a team to contribute relevant experience to the development of strategy. Of course as

100

members of the Board they had to supervise the Chief Executive but not in a way which made him less likely to solicit their support. One rule was to require that if a family let its shareholding drop below fifty per cent and subsequently a purchase by an unsuspecting member of the family took it back over fifty per cent a bid for the rest of the shareholding became mandatory. As with the Treasury so often the small print was all important and the vigilance of the Company Secretary crucial.

Prior to Big Bang I joined the West Midland & Wales Board of the National Westminster Bank as a non-executive director. The clearers were a functioning oligopoly. I remember at one meeting we were told that Barclays were proposing to open on a Saturday. This was most inconvenient and every effort would be made to persuade them not to. Success was anticipated.

They recruited numerate young men usually straight from the grammar schools and if they had not knocked any creativity out of them by their middle twenties it was not for want of trying. Not surprisingly those destined for senior posts often found it difficult to think out of the box. The banks, like the breweries, were property companies with a strong cash flow but their major asset was the inertia of their client base.

The comparison with the merchant banks was instructive. During my career we had in turn Schroders, Morgan Grenfell and Lazards as our advisors. We left Schroders because in the week before an issue of preference shares an old Etonian of exquisite languor infuriated our financial director by saying to the Board that he thought it could be got away but he would see. Morgan Grenfell we left because of a conflict of interest. Lazards eventually handled the sale of the company. Merchant bankers lived off their wits and success meant financial reward quite beyond what could be earned in a clearing bank.

I was told that when the Forte family received the bill from Warburgs for defending them from a takeover bid Rocco demanded to see the senior partner to challenge him to justify it. He was told to imagine that he had had the misfortune to have a fishbone lodged in his throat during lunch. A doctor is called and he is asked how much he is going to charge. Rather less than you are prepared to pay was the reply.

The regional boards of clearing banks were glorified lunch clubs to lock in important customers. They were useful networks. I found the conversation with other non-executive directors more rewarding than most of the routine presentations which we received. There were exceptions. I recall one which analysed the extent to which fraud was perfected by ethnic communities in different ways. For instance, the Nigerians concentrated on the credit card. The Commission for Racial Equality would have had a fit if such a paper were published today.

The two-day meetings for all directors at Heythrop were another matter. The non-executives represented a cross section of well informed people with whom it was useful to explore the nature of risk. Challenging the executive was our most important function. The last meeting that I attended I remember for its overall feeling of confidence. The bank was about to make a billion pounds for the first time and our Chairman, Robin Leigh Pemberton had just been appointed Governor of the Bank of England. It never crossed my mind that Nat West might be taken over by the Royal Bank of Scotland.

Years later I was interested to see that Derek Wanless, a former CEO, was the professional banker on the Board of Northern Rock. He had been asked to carry out an enquiry into the future of the NHS by Gordon Brown with whom he was evidently on good terms. I wonder at what point he warned No. 10 that Northern Rock was pursuing a high risk strategy which could all too quickly lead to disaster.

The advent of the big American and other international banks changed the City of London beyond recognition. To the old guard the barbarians were within the gates and to be seen as over-mighty subjects as unresponsive to the wider interests of the community as had been the barons of the old trade unions. Takeover and mergers which would once have been considered unthinkable proliferated. Everything and everyone could be bought and sold on borrowed money. The clearing banks rapidly deduced that their regional boards were a luxury which they could do without.

I also gave some time to Flemings as a director and later Chairman of one of their trusts. I saw my role as trying to frame the appropriate 'what if' question. The nature of risk in my own company was challenge enough; to review a portfolio was something else. The abiding pleasure of a visit to their offices was the collection of Scottish pictures which had been assembled through the Fine Arts Society. It was a classic demonstration of what could be delivered by one pair of eyes and a long-term relationship with dealers who understood both their market and the needs of their client.

When contemplating investment on my own behalf I always had one thought in the front of my mind; people make money in a wide range of ways but they spend it in a much narrower band: prime property, and works of art outstanding in their class, the best that you can afford and do not be afraid to pay for good advice. I have always found that property and works of art which fit this criterion have out performed the Stock Exchange and carried a real dividend in the pleasure that they bring. Liquidity should not be entirely forgotten.

The tax exemption enjoyed by the family house for capital gains tax makes it for most people their most important and rewarding investment. Understanding inflation and its future trend is crucial for individuals, companies and politicians. Without discipline in the Treasury and the Bank of England the best laid plans will be at risk. Controlling the rate of inflation is at the heart of good government. The Conservative party lost office largely because it forfeited its reputation for economic competence after Black Wednesday and too many voters experienced negative equity.

CHAPTER 19

English Heritage

A T A CONFERENCE for the Directors of the National Westminster Bank at Heythrop, John Smith came up to me and said, 'The Secretary of State has asked me to recommend somebody to chair English Heritage and I have suggested you.' I told him that I was flattered but would have to think about it. I went to see Jennifer Page who was then in charge to talk through what was involved. It required more time than I could afford to give. I made this clear. After Jocelyn Stevens who was Chairman of the Royal College of Art was appointed, Norman St John Stevas who would have liked the job, said to me, 'How could they have appointed piranha – the last time I saw him he had picked up a don and was shaking him.' I told him that I understood that the Secretary of State was looking for somebody to shake up English Heritage.

The National Trust had given me an understanding of what was involved in rescuing our secular heritage. I feared for our ecclesiastical. Would English Heritage be asked to fulfil a comparable role in the future? I remember suggesting to Margaret Thatcher when she was prepared to put up £200 million to acquire the Thyssen collection of Old Master paintings that such a sum would make a major contribution to the preservation of our great cathedrals. A number of bishops were not at that moment the flavour of the month and the proposal received short shrift.

Cathedrals always need money. Hereford was no exception. The west end had collapsed in times past for the lack of it. Before becoming an MP I had been Chairman of the Diocesan Board of Finance and involved in its first Appeal. The target was £110,000. I asked the Dean whether some money might be raised by increasing the rents of their property which had fallen well behind the market. He told me that he did not think that the Chapter would want to do that. 'What are you going to do about the Chapter?' I asked. 'Well' he replied, 'I look around the Chapter and think to myself while there is death there is hope.'

Herefordshire is not a rich county. The richest landowner was Charles Clore. Brigadier Clive, the Chairman of the Appeal, went to see him to ask for his support. He declined to give it but indicated that he would respond generously to an Appeal for a synagogue.

Despite disappointments we raised the money but it brought no more than temporary relief.

It was against this background some years later that the Bishop asked me to discuss the possible sale of the Mappa Mundi. It had hung largely unremarked in a transept and might not be missed. I asked Lord Gowrie, the Chairman of Sotheby's, what it might fetch; he told me that it could make anything between £7 million and £12 million: serious money which would make possible the endowment of the choir school and some much needed refurbishment of the cathedral. The issue became public and popular sentiment locally demanded that the Mappa be retained. I was asked to Chair the launch of a company to save it by selling facsimiles. I declined because I did not think it was a runner and I could not see from where else the cathedral was going to get the funds that it needed. In addition if the Mappa was sold it would very probably be bought by somebody from overseas and denied an export licence. It might then be purchased for the nation and perhaps returned to Hereford or at least loaned for a limited period, perhaps during the Three Choirs Festival. A solution to its future was provided by the generosity of Paul Getty but I still felt that the cathedral had missed out as it had before when it allowed the Gore Ouseley collection to go to Oxford.

Previous to the debate over the Mappa, controversy had raged over the removal of the Gilbert Scott screen which had been sent to the museum of Arts and Crafts in Coventry from which it was understood it could be recovered if sentiment changed. It transpired that Coventry had sold it and it had been lying in packing cases. The V&A was prepared to acquire it and display it and launched an Appeal for its restoration. The cathedral could not find any relevant records.

Our church buildings are the best memorials that we have to the changing nature of our history. In many ways they define it. Despite the destruction of so much during the Reformation and the Civil War they are our richest and most important inheritance and they are at risk. The war filled our churches. A secular media and neglect of religious education in our schools has emptied them. To the left the Anglican Church was the Tory Party at prayer, to Karl Marx religion the opiate of the people. The Anglican hierarchy demonstrated a massive crisis of confidence in itself. If the trumpet gives an uncertain sound ... retreat was in danger of becoming a rout. The Church Commissioners did no better. The Church is no longer in a position to protect its architectural inheritance.

The Church of England was created by a Welshman to protect his dynasty. Until the Accession of Henry Tudor any Welshman found within the walls of the City of Hereford was at risk of summary execution. The origins of its foundation were not noticeably divine but it has articulated in its use of the English language and in its music a richness in our cultural tradition without which we would be immeasurably the poorer. This too is now at risk: the unforgettable phrasing of the King James Bible and the masterpieces of our church music are in danger of becoming strangers in their own country.

Our centuries old Christian traditions are now under threat as never before from an increasingly secular culture driven by vocal minorities with no respect for our history. The charitable impulses which led to the creation of the majority of our schools and hospitals have their origins in the teachings of the New Testament. Take this away and perhaps the most important cement in our society will be dissolved and tensions exacerbated which could be difficult for any government to control.

CHAPTER 20

Herefordshire Health Authority

I WAS ASKED TO CHAIR the Herefordshire Health Authority. I accepted because I wanted to see Hereford provided with a new hospital and thought that my political experience might help to secure it. The city had three hospitals: the General, the County and the Victoria Eye. All were in need of replacement. There was a strong case for a greenfield site and a fresh start. Ease of access and speed of access were crucial considerations. Unfortunately, there was no agreement on whether Hereford should be bypassed on the east or the west and if early alternatives were to be provided to the existing Nissen huts which housed too many wards, it was clear that we would have to settle for less.

Sir James Ackers, the Chairman of the Regional Health Authority was very much in favour of one major scheme at a time rather than a step by step approach. We had to get our slot in the forward capital programme and a viable proposal in place. Beyond that there was the wider strategy for the county which I felt should be based on a ring of community hospitals – Leominster, Bromyard, Ledbury, Ross and perhaps Kington, to which patients could be released from the new acute hospital for rehabilitation, recuperation or terminal nursing. Working with the local authority these were constructed in Leomin-ster, Bromyard and Ross. Hereford required further thought. Ideally, there should be an enlarged GP practice alongside big enough to be able to afford the relevant IT which could make all the difference to the effective use of a doctor's time. The ability to process relevant information quickly and efficiently was also the key to identifying those at risk and improving their screening.

The Authority held regular meetings in public where important issues could be aired. These occasions could be used or misused for helpful exchanges or crude politicking. I remember being asked who represented the minority community on the board. I replied that I did not know in Herefordshire whether it was the English or the Welsh and never found out. The *Hereford Times* covered our agenda very fairly.

The eye hospital provided a service beyond the county to central Wales. Cataract operations brought immediate relief to many people and were an obvious priority. The building, though not ideal, was still serviceable.

The NHS was struggling with reform. It increasingly resembled the proverbial dinosaur with a small head in Whitehall and a huge body outside which employed more people than any other organisation in Europe except the Red Army. In management terms it was a disaster. Services were free at the point of delivery but nobody seemed to know what anything cost or to feel that there was any real incentive to control expenditure. No sanctions were visited on those who failed to turn up for their operation or who arrived in Accident & Emergency blind drunk and caused mayhem.

The NHS had the potential if not reformed to consume the whole resource of the nation. No other country in the developed world retained a mindset inherited from the 1940s. Private insurance played an important part in funding medical care on the Continent where standards were higher more often than not. Hereford did have a Nuffield hospital and my company was not alone in offering membership to its employees. This relieved some of the pressure on the NHS but it was on a small scale. People were living longer and families increasingly unwilling to look after elderly relatives. Private nursing homes were essential to complement cash-strapped social services. Drugs were becoming more expensive. A new level of sophistication was being reached in IT which meant more investment in management, software and training. More skilled nurses were needed but not at the expense of those natural carers on the wards whose contribution was too often undervalued. They provided the sympathetic understanding which lies at the core of nursing. Some of them were not going to pass exams but they were vital to the care of the elderly.

The task of the executive was not an easy one. They had to run the existing facilities and at the same time plan for the future against a background of ever-changing approaches in Whitehall. There was never enough money to go round despite annual increases. Too often some emergency would require time and cash which had not been anticipated. In the background were a moral maze and a political minefield. AIDS was taking its toll. What should the response be to the health risks associated with anal intercourse practised by homosexuals? Afflictions such as motor neurone disease ran a predictable course at some point during which the patient might request that their end be hastened; how far could the medical team go? Doctors too often had to play God at the beginning and end of life. Beyond charity and common sense could there, should there be new rules? Should the Living Will be given statutory backing? Should doctors following their conscience be at risk of a criminal prosecution?

Meetings of the Regional Health Authority touched on some of these issues but they were really for Parliament. Even there, informed debate was too often lacking. Members of Parliament were frightened off by elements among their constituents committed to their own viewpoints which could be extreme and by the usually unhelpful interventions of the tabloid press.

We achieved our place in the forward capital programme for the hospital but it was put on hold until the details of the new Private Finance Initiative had been finalised. The authority was also to be split into three parts and my job disappeared. I was delighted when Brian Nelson agreed to become Chairman of the new acute hospital. He had the expertise not easily found to carry through the challenge of the PFI procedures and deliver the new building while maintaining a level of service. He did so brilliantly.

I had one regret. Before John Major, as Prime Minister, visited Bulmers, I asked to see the Chairman of the Party. There was a considerable delay before I was able to do so. I remarked that in my day if a Member, or former Member, wanted a word it happened very quickly. He responded that the Magic Circle had worked for me but not for him and it was dead. I told him that unless the plans for Hereford hospital were presented positively and the Prime Minister's visit was a perfect opportunity, Colin Shepherd would lose his seat. Nothing happened and Hereford fell to the Liberal Democrats. The Party seemed to have a death wish; so much for my political experience.

CHAPTER 21

Earth in the Balance

I WAS APPROACHED BY THE Principal of the Holme Lacy Agricultural
College to lead an appeal to save it. We discussed the current
situation which did not look hopeful. There was, however, a totally
different scenario. Holme Lacy was the greatest house surviving from
the seventeenth century in Herefordshire. It was situated in a grade
one park and had once had an outstanding garden. It had been used
as a hospital in recent years. As Chairman of the Health Authority I
had paid for it to be re-roofed before it was returned to the county
council to whom it had been given by the Wills family. They then
sold it. Two hotel companies had got into financial difficulty trying
to restore it further. The building was now well suited for educational
purposes.

Lord Scudamore had been a pioneer in the making of cider of the
highest quality. The Red Streak apple, the White Faced cattle and
the Wye salmon were defining symbols of the county of Hereford.
Could all this be brought together to provide a new college of
sustainable agriculture?

I believed that Al Gore's book, *Earth in the Balance*, rehearsed the
scale and variety of the threats facing the planet in a way which no
serious politician could ignore. As governments began to face up to
these issues they would be increasingly wanting to educate the public
about the consequences of their actions. I gave John Birt who was
then the Director General of the BBC a copy and asked him to
consider whether the corporation might provide even one hour a
week of prime time television helping people to understand some of
the issues involved. What was meant by global warming? How fast
was the polar ice cap melting? What was the ozone layer? What was

its connection with cancer? What were the arguments for and against nuclear, wind and tide as sources for the generation of energy?

As a public broadcaster I felt that the BBC had a duty to pose such questions and provide relevant information. Unless this was done, politicians had little hope of obtaining acceptance when they wanted to promote the long-term interests of the country over the short-term satisfaction of the consumer. Aviation fuel was not taxed and yet aircraft were major polluters; cheap food could be brought in from all over the world by the supermarkets which destroyed farmers' livelihoods. What was the true cost of convenience?

I asked the American Ambassador in London after dinner whether he had considered the Vice President's views: he might well believe that Al Gore would shortly become the President. It was clear that it was not front of mind. I asked him which he thought would do more for humanity, that the Vatican re-wrote *Humanae Vitae* (contraceptives were obviously important in the fight against AIDS) or the US put up the price of gas. He laughed and said, 'I can sure tell you that we are not going to put up the price of gas.'

I was amazed when I was in Washington watching the TV debates between the Presidential candidates that Al Gore did not talk more about his concerns, given that his book opens with an attack on George Bush senior for not taking the environmental lead at the Rio Conference. He compared him with Woodrow Wilson abandoning the League of Nations and opening the way to the Second World War. The consequences this time could be eco-catastrophe. It became increasingly clear that politicians were happier to talk about these issues than to take action which might undermine their political support.

It had taken the German armies to go into action before the British population really woke up to the need for re-armament, it had taken the winter of discontent before they accepted the need for trade union reform; what had to happen in the form of an ecological disaster for the threats to our environment to be taken seriously enough for the necessary steps to be implemented or would it all be too late?

John Birt asked me to dinner with Robin Butler, the Head of the Civil Service, and I asked him where at the interface between the higher Civil Service and Oxbridge these issues were considered, the threats and opportunities ranked and solutions proposed. It did not appear to be happening. I knew one Permanent Secretary who regarded the Prime Minister's adviser on the environment as a nuisance which he could do without. Were Civil Servants reflecting the reluctance of their masters to get involved? History may come to judge.

The Principal of Holme Lacy College responded to this scenario enthusiastically and we set up the Bulmer Foundation to support the initiative. Prince Charles had become the largest landowner in Herefordshire and his approach was highly compatible. Jonathan Porritt, the Prime Minister's Special Adviser, was the leading crusader for a wake-up call. He was very supportive. Government was increasingly talking sustainability. Could it all be made to happen?

CHAPTER 22

Monopolies Commission

THE CIDER MARKET returned to growth in the 1990s as a result of increased advertising and the introduction of new products. Taunton, the brewers' cider company was acquired by Matthew Clark. Matthew Clark was a well-established wine shipper, best known as the agent for Martell brandy. After, amid much acrimony, the Martell family sold out for a very high price. Matthew Clark lost the agency. Francis Gordon Clark discussed with me whether we might be interested in acquiring his company. We were not. In due course it became the vehicle into which Michael Cottrell, the chairman of Taunton, and previously the managing director of Courage, transferred the company. He became its Chairman. The shareholders in Taunton did well, those in Matthew Clark less well. Michael said to me that he expected life would go on as if nothing had happened. We would each hold on to our existing brewery relationships. I suggested that he stopped thinking like a brewer and told him that the Monopolies Commission had changed the rules of engagement. We should each spend our money promoting our brands and think twice before competing on discounts. This approach would best benefit the industry. Michael died suddenly and the future of Matthew Clark was once more being questioned.

From the time of the MMC report we thought long and hard about acquiring through the market what had to a considerable extent been taken from us by unfair commercial practice. We could not expect any compensation but could we buy the company? We sought advice from the DTI. It was, I was told, a twenty-six year old woman who decreed that we were not part of the long drinks market. This meant that we would have to pass all the competition hurdles leading perhaps to a reference to the Monopolies Commission if we wished to proceed with a bid. The outcome was uncertain and it would put Bulmers into limbo for months. The combined company would have been smaller than any of the major brewers but it would have had the resource to pursue a credible international strategy.

The DTI could not get its mind round the changing nature of competition in the world. In some product areas like aeroplane manufacture continental scale was necessary. The UK was fast falling behind in many markets because it lacked the size required to compete effectively. The DTI resisted the concept of national champion. It also expected the rest of the world to play cricket. British businessmen could land in gaol for bribery. I remember one managing director telling me that he had been asked to quote for a power station over the Russian border from Iran. The deal was factored out of Teheran and there was a tariff showing from the Prime Minister down who got what 'commission'.

The DTI advice seemed to be that if you were going to fish in murky waters you got a Frenchman or an Italian to do it for you.

One outcome of the Monopolies Commission report which was evidently not foreseen was the formation of ever larger pub groups. The suppliers found their margins squeezed. In addition the super-markets became ever more powerful and demanded that their own label products replaced those of the advertised brand to a greater extent. Price was more important than value and too many people did not recognise the distinction.

A former chairman of Taunton who had been managing director of Berger Paints once said to me, 'It is only too easy to compete the profit out of an industry. I have learnt my lesson.' As Matthew Clark lost market share it forgot this and increasingly sought to maintain its position by spending more on discounts and less on advertising. It was not a credible strategy and in due course the company was taken over by the American company Canandaigua controlled by the Sands family.

John Rudgard had done a good job building the Strongbow brand and developing the recovery of the cider market. Bulmers' share price rose year on year. We now approached another crossroads. He was nearing retirement and future earnings growth looked as though it was going to depend more and more on success overseas. We had renewed talks with Guinness but they did not lead to an offer. Our share price was high and it would have been difficult for the Board not to recommend an offer which represented a reasonable premium.

Will Samuel had joined our Board as a non-executive director when he was head of Corporate Finance at Shroders. He was to be the Board's preference to succeed me as Chairman. Alistair Mitchell Innes, the Deputy Chairman who was also retiring, took charge of the search for a new Chief Executive using the head-hunters, Egon Zehnder. Mike Hughes was appointed. He had originally been recruited by Ernest Saunders from Coca-Cola where he was their European Marketing Director to strengthen Guinness and he had valuable American experience.

He had a good hand to play. The duty on cider in America had been reduced from its champagne level by a factor of five largely as the result of the Irish lobby. Senators Moynihan and Kennedy engineered the change which was welcomed in the Boston bars. We purchased the American Hard Cider Company from an Irishman against strong competition from Cantrell & Cochrane and South African Breweries. Cantrell & Cochrane were the owners of the Bulmer brand in Ireland of which they had made a great success. What sort of deal could, should be sought?

The competition in the UK was in disarray. The key task was to restore margins by making Strongbow a must-stock brand and by improving the distribution chain perhaps in co-operation with Guinness. This could lead to being asked to handle an important beer brand looking for a new distributor following the break up of major brewing companies. New product development remained important. In South Africa and Australia there were new opportunities to consider. There was also the possibility of merging the company with one or perhaps two companies of equal weight to create the necessary critical mass to exploit the opportunities created by the changes brought about by the MMC. Exploratory talks had been held.

CHAPTER 23

Studley Royal

B EFORE I RETIRED Susie and I had considered spending half the year in Australia after I did so. Every year we went to Sydney it was getting better, every year we returned to London it was getting worse. Sydney Harbour had been given a focus by the Opera House, Australian arts were thriving, the range and the excellence of the food and wine and the views across the water provided a combination that was only beaten by Venice to which we continued to make an annual pilgrimage. We acquired clearance for dual nationality and came close to buying a property on Darling Point. In the end family consider-ations, my mother's descent into Alzheimer's and concern for the dogs made us think again.

We moved to Studley Royal in Yorkshire. Bulmers had been established in Durham, Yorkshire and Northumberland before the Norman invasion. Of a warlike disposition they were valued for their ability to defend the frontier against incursions from the Scots. In due course two of their most important castles, Brauncepeth and Sheriff Hutton passed to the Nevills through marriage and thence to the House of York. After the Howards rose to prominence they fought alongside in Ireland and on the borders and at the Battle of Flodden left the flower of the Scottish aristocracy dead upon the field. On the accession of the Tudors and Henry VIII's attack on the Catholic Church many Northern families did not know where their true loyalties lay. The betrayal of so many of them by the Duke of Norfolk after the Pilgrimage of Grace led to their downfall. The grounds of Studley Royal include the ruins of Fountains Abbey. I used to sit on Anne Boleyn's seat looking down on the River Skell and the ruins of that great monastic house and reflect that if she had produced a healthy male child how different might have been the course of history.

I had been on the Executive of the National Trust when the estate was acquired. The house had been burnt down at the end of the war and the family had moved into the High Stables designed by Colen Campbell for William Aislabie. His father John had been Queen Anne's Treasurer at the time of the South Sea Bubble from which he had made a fortune. When the scandal broke, he was put into the Tower from which in due course he bought himself out to spend the rest of his life creating a great garden. Susie's parents had been given a house to restore by Rennie Hoare at Stourhead, another of the outstanding gardens of the Enlightenment. The Hoares had been bankers to the Aislabies and although the pattern of the planting was to develop the two gardens in very different ways both found their inspiration in the classical world. Henry Hoare told me that they had built their business in the eighteenth century by always having a member of the family available through the night to settle gambling debts. Sadly it was such debts that led to the break up of the Studley estates.

Paul Sykes who had made a fortune out of the Meadowhall Shopping Centre in Sheffield employed a talented team to restore the High Stables. The National Trust had not acquired the house and could not have done a better job. Paul found the Trust a difficult neighbour for reasons that I came to understand and took the decision to sell to us.

When I first became involved in the National Trust it was amateur in the best sense: it was a crusade of like-minded people to defend important elements in our heritage. Its very success demanded that it became more professional. Pat Gibson introduced Angus Stirling to achieve this. When Pat was succeeded by Jennifer Jenkins she found herself attacked by David Clark, the Shadow Secretary for the Environment and my opposite number on the Executive. He had been born in the stables of a great house and challenged the role of the Trust in enabling the families who had made over their homes to the Trust to go on living there.

I had warned Jennifer when we had lunch together before she took up her appointment that I thought that the chemistry of the Trust was very fragile. It depended for its unity on a generation which was disappearing and on retaining the goodwill of families still living in houses where they retained some of the most important contents. I remember the consternation when the Uppark commodes appeared in Sotheby's.

The membership of the Trust grew dramatically. It far exceeded the combined membership of all political parties and became increasingly urban in its composition. This made it far more vulnerable to the class warriors who had infiltrated the Ramblers, the RSPCA, and the RSPB, when hunting became an issue. This divided the Trust in a way which did it great damage and demonstrated as clearly as the reaction to the death of Diana the extent to which we had become two nations but in this instance town and country rather than young and old.

I told Charles Nunneley when he became Chairman that I did not know whether to congratulate him or to commiserate with him. To try to steer an organisation when it was a lot harder to express a value judgement which you felt confident commanded the support of your audience was an exceptional challenge. Once you sought to outlaw what the law allowed you had crossed the Rubicon.

The time devoted to the bill to outlaw hunting demonstrated on the one hand the feebleness of the House of Commons in the hands of people who, deprived of the red meat of Socialism, saw it as some sort of retribution for the defeat of the miners and, on the other, the increasing role of the House of Lords in defending the country from a naked form of fascism. Scotland had demonstrated the futility of it all. However hard Labour ministers might try to make out an argument about animal welfare it was manifestly fraudulent. One friend who was stopped in the street and asked to sign a petition against hunting enquired why the man thought the fox might benefit from being poisoned, snared or shot and wounded rather than killed quickly by its natural enemy was told, 'Fuck the fox – it's the toffs we are after!' Tony Blair asked at dinner why hunting was important replied, 'It isn't, and I wish it would go away.' His wife spat at him across the table, 'Tony, you are pledged.'

A Welsh hill farmer was reported to have gone up to a Labour minister when he was being shown some forestry and enquired, 'Which of you is the minister?' The minister smiled and looked pleased. The farmer said to him, 'Are you going to stop the fox killing my lambs? Do you see what it is I have in my hand? It is a box of matches Boyo,' and he pointed at the trees. Much of the country became a no-go area for Government ministers.

From the end of the Second World War the population became increasingly divorced from the countryside. Farmers who had worked hard to feed the nation during the German blockade were encouraged, only to be told when their incomes rose that they were feather-bedded. They were given grants to drain the land and remove the hedgerows to create fields big enough to benefit from ever larger machinery only to be dismissed as environmental vandals. Numbers employed dropped continuously.

The Trust found it harder to recruit people who understood both the natural world and the demands of the urban membership. Staff went from one meeting to another trying to balance the competing claims of the farmer and the archaeologist, the ornithologist and the landscape architect, the botanist and the forester and the ever present bills associated with the maintenance of the country house and its contents. The mushrooming demands of a multi-tiered bureaucracy producing a new regulation a day on everything from the ladder to be used by a window cleaner to access for the handicapped were an added burden. The Trust seemed increasingly to resemble local government in its inability to allow an individual to get on with the job. Fewer and fewer people seemed to understand the value of money and the checks on whether it was spent responsibly were inadequate. Costs were no longer supervised by people accustomed to signing cheques on their own behalf and there was less and less lateral thinking. The values of the country gave way to those of the town. Few of those who demanded the end of hunting had the slightest understanding of the contribution made to the ecology of the countryside by the concern of landowners to preserve their traditional sports. The Trust was increasingly questioned by those who had once been its more enthusiastic supporters.

CHAPTER 24

Retirement

I T IS NORMAL ON RETIREMENT to take a back seat and keep your mouth shut. Your successor is now at the helm and must be allowed to set the course. I was fortunate that John Norton had joined the Board as a non-executive director. He had been the Senior Partner of Binder Hamlyn before its merger with Arthur Andersen and had thirty years' experience of the company. He had been an important part of the team during the public issue and unlike many accountants combined competence and a wider vision with humour and a shrewd understanding of human nature. He had been a friend of Andrew Harding. He and Alistair Mitchell Innes were a great support through the trial to come.

Mike Hughes made a good start. He provided strong leadership in consolidating the primacy of the Strongbow brand in the domestic cider market and in developing an international business. He was unlucky in his choice of Leeds United to carry the Strongbow logo as some of its key players seemed more determined to pick fights with immigrants after hours than to score goals.

In Australia the introduction of a General Sales Tax threatened the profitability of cider as had happened before in a different way in the UK. The contrast between the way in which the Australian and the British Government responded to a request for dialogue could not have been more stark. In Canberra the Treasury, unlike their Whitehall counterparts, were prepared to discuss in some detail a financial model and to accept advice from the Department of Primary Products on the value of cider as an end user of apples. At that time we were sponsoring the English cricket team which the Australians had no difficulty in defeating. John Howard, the Prime Minister, thought that perhaps we deserved a break and we were granted concessions which made the tax changes manageable. Alistair Goodlad, a former colleague in the House of Commons, had just become our High Commissioner and he was extremely helpful.

Mike Hughes did not grasp the extent to which politics and the taxation of alcohol were deeply intertwined. He was also reluctant to delegate sufficiently to our Australian management. Mistakes were made which might otherwise have been avoided.

In the US the opportunity for (hard) cider created by the dramatic fall in the level of duty cried out to be exploited. It seemed that no sooner had the change been introduced than the drinks market was swept by the success of ready-to-drink products which were spirit based. Cider could not finance the advertising required which might have delivered success and Mike Hughes apparently did not recognise the urgent need for a partnership with Cantrell & Cochrane. He played hard to get and lost out.

In South Africa he was offered an apparently advantageous opportunity to reacquire our former cider interests from Diageo (Guinness). I was against the deal but the Board thought, since not a lot of money was involved, he should be allowed to back his judgement. It was another mistake. I had feared that it would require Lonhro skills to obtain distribution against South African Breweries and we did not possess them. So it proved.

In the UK he acquired a beer wholesaling business to improve our distribution and to attract a major beer brand. It was a sound operation but not more without a significant lift in turnover which was not achieved.

Organisations do not have ambitions, people do. Mike Hughes wanted to make a lot of money quickly and thought he could do it easily. I believed that he did not give sufficient attention to the fundamentals and when the income from the new acquisitions failed to deliver as forecast, the company's gearing started to look too high for comfort.

At this point I said to Roger Cooke, the other family member, that I thought that we had too many eggs in one basket. It appeared to me he had always been reluctant to consider the duty of a director to all shareholders if the sale of the company was an issue. I had urged him some years earlier to talk on a regular basis to the shareholders that he represented about the future of the company so that they should be aware of the threats and opportunities facing it if an important decision had to be made. He had found this difficult. His senior cousin said to me, 'Roger has a hard time, we are an anarchic lot.' Under the rules of the Stock Exchange once a company is deemed to be in play a family director is prevented from divulging information to other members of the family not available to all shareholders. Too many members of the family started from behind and never caught up.

I expressed the need for an exit strategy to the Board. This was agreed and Lazards were consulted. I also believed that if Bulmers were to be taken over it should be by a British company. That was likely to mean Scottish & Newcastle. An approach was made to their Chairman Brian Stewart who after his own consultations said that he wished to enter negotiations. This was in the July just after the company had produced its annual results. Mike Hughes had had to issue profit warnings earlier in the year but then told the Board just before the AGM in September that the company was in breach of its bank covenants. He had to go. Will Samuel demonstrated his technical competence in handling the sale of the company which had become all but inevitable. Miles Templeman, a former Chief Executive of Whitbread, took over the day to day running of the company whilst Marcus Agius of Lazards conducted an auction which produced a far better result than the City had anticipated.

After S&N took over, it was inevitable that there would be many job losses but at least they were in areas of readily transferable skills. The contracts with the fruit growers were maintained and the commitments to pensioners sustained. It remained to be seen whether

S&N could make Strongbow the international brand which it had the potential to become. It was all a terrible disappointment after the high hope of two years earlier.

Looking back I ask myself whether if the Treasury had handled their tax increases on cider with greater competence, if the power of the retailer over the manufacturer through oligopoly had been challenged earlier by the MMC and if the DTI had accepted that cider was part of the long drinks market, how differently things might have turned out.

The sale of the company put money into the hands of the family shareholders and I can hear my great-grandfather praying, 'At all times of our wealth, Good Lord deliver us,' and my grandfather's reminder, 'The City is full of good bookmakers but bloody bad at breeding horses'.

Family control can have the merit of keeping a significant company out of the hands of the speculators. Well led, it can put the long term over the short term and guarantee on-going investment in a community and beyond. Its importance as an employer can be all too clear. Estate Duty may represent a death sentence.

I have seen at first hand that more people are destroyed by a great inheritance than enabled. Drugs, sex, gambling, depression brought on by ennui, blind extravagance are all too familiar stories. On the other hand money can deliver independence and freedom to pursue a more fulfilling life – as so often, it is a question of balance.

In America, business success is lauded unlike in the UK where it is too often resented; education, the arts and medicine all benefit massively from endowments as a result. Would that it might follow here more often than it does.

CHAPTER 25

New Labour

THE FORMATION OF New Labour was the ultimate tribute to Margaret Thatcher. Old Labour had proved unelectable. After Tony Blair won the election in 1997 I looked at the names of those who would hold senior positions in the new Government. Only a small minority had any ministerial experience. Many of them I remembered as student agitators, ban-the-bombers and defenders of the indefensible when it came to trade union malpractice; high tax and spend to a man. Their attitude to Europe and the US had changed and changed again. What had they learnt?

I enquired of a Labour MP who was expecting to hold office whether he was looking forward to it. 'Not really,' he replied. 'We have this huge constitutional agenda which we had not thought through, we are at least as divided over Europe as you are and until we are in place we don't know whether we are Old Labour or New Labour.'

Their first act was to make the Governor of the Bank responsible for the control of inflation. This recognised their past failure to run the economy successfully and was eminently sensible; equally the decision to stick to Kenneth Clark's spending plans. There was no going back on the Conservative reform of the law governing trade unions but the new Government signed up to the social contract and the minimum wage. The true nature of the international competition in prospect from the Far East was not understood. The trade unions still had to be appeased.

Tony Blair enjoyed great goodwill at home and abroad. The Conservative Parliamentary Party had not distinguished itself. Its divisions over our future relationship with Europe and the private failings of too many individual members took their toll. Who could reasonably deny that it was a time for change?

There was nonetheless some unfinished business to complete. The key to peace in Northern Ireland lay through the White House. The IRA was largely financed by Americans and Dublin would listen to Washington. The talks initiated by John Major were carried through to the Belfast Agreement.

Progress to 'ever closer union' in Europe favoured, it was thought, by Tony Blair, since it got him off so many hooks, lay through the euro and the break up of the United Kingdom. Labour only exceptionally achieved a majority in England and relied on Scotland and Wales to gain power. Wales by the narrowest of margins voted for devolution, Scotland more enthusiastically. Plans for regional government in England were prepared but could not attract support.

'Cool Britannia' was the slogan under which the past was to be buried and the constitution apparently vandalised by the Prime Minister who appeared to parade his ignorance of history as a virtue. The House of Commons was ignored. It ranked behind Rupert Murdoch. His MPs had to be 'on message'. Procedural reform deprived the opposition of its one effective weapon: time. Bills, often badly drafted, were subject to the guillotine and the House of Lords often misrepresented if it subjected legislation to the proper scrutiny that it had been denied in the Commons. The House of Lords had defied reform for nearly a century. In my time it failed to make progress because of an unlikely alliance between Enoch Powell and Tony Benn. Robert Cranborne struck a deal to preserve (temporarily) the hereditary principle which probably suited the Prime Minister who did not want the elected Chamber favoured by a majority of his MPs who had not got their minds around the new division of powers which this would involve. Patronage was the key to freeing New Labour from the trade union cheque book. Even Lloyd George looked like a beginner when it came to the number of peers created by Tony Blair. The office of Lord Chancellor was to be abolished by press release and the Civil Service subjected to unprecedented political pressure. Power was dispensed from sofas in Number Ten. The Prime Minister demanded eye-catching initiatives and photo opportunities. Neither was a substitute for good government.

'Tough on crime, tough on the causes of crime' was an oft repeated mantra. The root of most crime lay in poor parenting and drug abuse. A drug tsar was appointed who made little impression. The underclass in the council estate expanded. Since teenage pregnancy out of marriage met with no public disapproval and was rewarded with housing and maintenance it was not surprising that it was to rise to the highest level in Europe. The attempt to make errant fathers pay the costs of their children was another massive failure. Divorce levels continued to increase. The tax system did nothing to encourage marriage. The Chancellor appeared to want to force mothers out to work. Immigrants were encouraged because they voted Labour and Labour MPs seemed to spend much of their time soliciting grants and subsidy for their supporters. Small wonder that the cost of Social Services spiralled and with it fraud which went largely unchecked.

'Education, education, education' was another mantra. The comprehensive was sacred to Old Labour despite massive evidence that it deprived bright children from poor backgrounds from realising their potential. The destruction of the grammar school and the abolition of the assisted places scheme were the product of socialist dogma which demanded that nobody was better than anybody else and of ideologues for whom competition and the pursuit of excellence were anathema. A friend of mine who took early retirement from the Department of Education described it as 'institutionally socialist'. It worked happily with Labour-controlled councils in concealing the true state of affairs in their failing comprehensive schools. It consumed far too high a proportion of the education budget and brought few obvious benefits. It increasingly resembled an Orwellian world in which failure was described as success as examinations pass marks were lowered and the curriculum dumbed down. New criteria had to be invented to get more children from state schools into Oxbridge. The proportion had fallen sharply with the closure of grammar schools.

I was sitting next to Roy Jenkins at lunch after Gordon Brown made his seemingly unjustified accusations against Oxford for refusing admission to one of his constituents. As Chancellor of the University Roy understood the extent to which Oxbridge was under-funded and losing out to the best American universities. He accepted the charge that he and a lot of his former Labour colleagues had got into Oxbridge from grammar schools and then raised the drawbridge. Comprehensive education had failed to live up to expectations. The large number of immigrants in some cities speaking many different languages had made the teachers' task far more difficult as had the growing shortcomings of too many parents. Poor teachers could not be removed and the authority of headteachers to exclude was too often undermined by political correctness. He saw no quick solutions.

In America the best universities received great support from their alumni. Family continuity is encouraged; not in my old college. After a cousin had been refused entry he got an Exhibition at New College. He wrote to Kings asking if in view of the long association of the family with the college he might be accepted as a Commoner. He received a letter back inviting him to see a psychiatrist. Not surprisingly when requests for money were received at a later date from the College the reaction was not as warm as it would otherwise have been.

Tony Blair had to give some jobs in his cabinet to Old Labour stalwarts. I viewed Dobson at Health and Prescott at Transport as manifestly ill-equipped to introduce the changes required to meet the challenges ahead in the NHS and in the road and rail network. It was no surprise that they failed.

The countryside was never understood by the Labour party. Tied cottages, the right to roam and animal rights were the only subjects in which an interest was taken. When foot and mouth broke out the response was a costly shambles and only sorted as a result of the intervention of the Army. DEFRA continued to bombard farmers with forms of such complexity that nobody could be found to explain them. Animal rights terrorists were not pursued with the full rigour of the law. Powers were taken to transfer major planning decisions involving new housing development or detention centres for illegal immigrants away from those likely to be most affected. Parish councillors had to declare their shareholdings thereby, it was hoped, discouraging Conservatives.

For many voters Tony Blair's undertaking not to increase income tax was the clearest break with the past. Gordon Brown's raid on pension funds and a windfall tax on utility companies set the trend to raise money in other ways. Stealth taxes were not the stuff of headlines.

Low interest rates encouraged borrowing for consumption and housing at a level which could not be sustained over the long term. Rising house prices generated a feel-good factor which prompted accelerating debt through an explosion of credit cards. At the same time the Chancellor sought to borrow off balance sheet. The Private Finance Initiative stored up charges for the future which were not understood. Similarly, more and more people were recruited into the public sector where their future inflation-proof entitlement would be a charge over a sharply declining number of tax payers. This was often given as a justification for immigration without the higher costs on the infrastructure or social services being taken into account. The reasons why our education system failed to produce the skills which now allegedly had to be imported were not addressed.

Tony Blair had promised to reform the public sector. This involved challenging the Old Labour power base in the trade unions and was resisted by enough of his MPs to mean that reform could only be taken through Parliament with Conservative support. Had the Conservative leadership supported him wholeheartedly over foundation hospitals, new forms of school and university top-up fees it would have served the country better and probably torn the Parliamentary Labour party apart.

Labour was re-elected largely on the basis that it needed more time to deliver, and the lack of an effective opposition. Its second term saw a return to tax and spend and the dissipation of the Thatcher legacy. Increasingly the British economy came to resemble the continental in building up pension and welfare benefits which could not be afforded. The Government did not want to risk a referendum on the euro, nor to challenge the public sector workers whose productivity seldom increased in line with higher pay and too often declined. Immigration, much of it illegal, rose out of control and many of our major cities continued to be deserted by the middle class, a significant number of whom despairing of the mother country, went to live abroad. The working class preferred their own kind as neighbours, but were constantly lectured by the BBC thought-police that they were racist to do so. Few of their critics lived surrounded by the drug dealer and the ghetto blaster. Pensioners, whose rate bills rose faster than their income saw no personal benefit from the gender-awareness officer in the swimming pool or the inter-faith counsellor in the gay/lesbian bereavement centre, or most of the countless other Lib/Lab inventions recorded in the advertisement columns of *The Guardian*.

Manufacturing industry continued to shed jobs and the income generated by the City of London became increasingly important. It was dominated by the large American banks whose rewards represen-ted in Dr Johnson's phrase, 'Riches beyond the dreams of avarice'. We had been going to buy a house in Cornwall from a friend who was short of money. He telephoned to say that he was going to let us down. The next day we read in the *Financial Times* that his brother stood to benefit by £90 million from three years' employment at Goldman Sachs. City bonuses drove property at the top end of the market to unprecedented heights and the trickle-down effect meant that more women stayed at work and delayed having babies until they could afford a starter home. Another undesirable feature was the growth of asset stripping; leveraged buy-outs of increasing sophistication led inexorably to the junk bond. In America a few crooks went to gaol but the majority did not. Corporate excess might prove to be America's Achilles heel if not effectively constrained. So it proved.

The destruction of the twin towers in New York changed the world, not least for Tony Blair. American support had been key to a solution of the Northern Ireland question – now it was impossible for the IRA to return to bombing the British mainland without the Sinn Fein leaders, Adams and McGuinness, losing all credibility. The Americans now needed support. Tony Blair, ever anxious to prevent the Conservative opposition getting too close to a Republican president humiliated many of his own supporters by appearing to them to become George Bush's poodle. The Parliamentary Labour party were sold the dodgy dossier which invited them to support war on Iraq. It remained deeply divided. Demonstrations against the American intervention in Iraq were led in London by a Labour mayor whose support relied significantly on the Moslem vote.

Labour's failure to control immigration or to tackle fundamentalism in the mosques in its constituencies made it look vulnerable. A former Labour MP and chat show host, Robert Kilroy Silk, set up his own party and challenged the BBC and other commentators to defend such Moslem fundamentalist beliefs as the execution of homosexuals and the stoning to death of women taken in adultery. Interviewers fled. The Church of England skulked in its tent. Multiculturalism was on the defensive. It was now possible to express points of view which would previously have awarded anybody articulating them pariah status.

The Iraq war and the death of Dr Kelly were Tony Blair's Westland moment. He was not, however, challenged by Gordon Brown with whom his relationship remained troubled. The Hutton enquiry was regarded by many as a whitewash but it did, however, reveal a great deal about the way the Prime Minister conducted his

Government, often excluding the Cabinet from important debate and preventing civil servants from keeping proper records. The seemingly shameless behaviour of Alistair Campbell, the Prime Minister's Press Secretary, demanded that he faded from the scene.

I once met Kelvin McKenzie, the then editor of the *Sun* at dinner. Whenever a politician's name came up his response always seemed to be, 'What have we got on them then?' The Leader of the Lib Dems was 'Pantsdown (Ashdown) – we are working on more of the birds he screwed but none of them have croaked yet.' The only person he seemed to respect was Mr Murdoch.

This form of journalism had been fed by Labour in opposition and it played an important part in diminishing the respect in which MPs were held. If the price of becoming a minister was to have your private life subjected to the prurient scrutiny of the Murdoch press, many competent people would stay out of politics. A number of Labour MPs were hoisted on their own petard.

The Lib Dem flirtation with Labour did not deliver PR, the bait held out for co-operation. Nevertheless, a partnership was forged in the devolved Scottish Assembly which was to produce an administration of notable incompetence. The cost of the parliamentary building ten times over the original budget reflected the general lack of control. The output of the Scottish NHS where the old union attitudes and power prevailed was among the worst in Europe. The attack on Highland landlords on whom much of the local economy depended reflected the mix of prejudice, ignorance and socialist sentimentality that had been demonstrated in the Commons debate on hunting. Why Scottish MPs should be allowed to vote either on hunting in England or the NHS in England was not justified nor could it be. The Lothian question remained unanswered and the electoral system so biased in Labour's favour that an equality of votes produced a majority for them of between sixty and seventy seats.

The war in Iraq cost the Labour party votes and benefited the Lib Dems who remained the party of choice when it came to protest. To be a British soldier in Basra was a confusing experience. My son, who served there, told me:

> We all knew that no member of the Cabinet had ever put on a uniform. We received no clear briefing on their strategy. We were asked to turn Iraqis into policemen. We never knew whose side they were really on – only that their first instinct on taking a person into custody was to beat them up. If we stepped out of line we could end up accused of war crimes.

A friend of his who volunteered for the police force on his return to the UK was turned down. Policemen, particularly in London, were selected according to a points system based on political correctness against which military training and a record in the field counted for little. Under Labour violent crime escalated. Police effectiveness was seriously reduced by form-filling which reflected their pc agenda. It was hardly surprising that if a constable saw a Jamaican high on ganga with every chance a weapon in his pocket bearing down on him he would be on his guard – that did not make him institutionally racist. Of course a balance had to be struck but the outcome too often deprived the ordinary citizen of the protection that was their due. A disproportionate amount of mugging and murder was carried out by the ethnic community.

The police also had to cope with a steady increase in bad behaviour in the young. Britain had the highest rate of teenage pregnancy and sexual disease in Europe. The lack of discipline in the home and too often in school, the example set on the football field and in the pop world had created a culture which was seen by many as the most degenerate in the West. Sections of the media too often seemed to set out to encourage it. It was a far cry from the world of my youth.

History may judge the Blair Government more harshly than the electorate when it was returned for a third term. More people in England voted Conservative than for Labour but most people did not vote at all. Tony Blair had long recognised that the truth usually turns out to be Conservative. He continued to bluff his way avoiding the hard choices required to reform the public sector. He did not send his children to the local comprehensive, nor did a third of his MPs, many of whom educated their children privately. He made speeches about the environment before and after the election but in between it was all too difficult. Transport went nowhere. How to pay for pensions and the NHS in the future was kicked into the long grass. Immigration and crime figures were fudged. A vote on the euro and the European constitution put back. Belfast was once more a problem. Having apparently betrayed David Trimble to appease IRA/Sinn Fein he had only himself to blame when Ian Paisley spoke for Protestant Northern Ireland. At a personal and public level the country was sliding deeper into debt.

The kindest thing to be said of the Conservative party is that it had been resting. Its track record was dismal. The Parliamentary party too often did not pull together or give of its best. Michael Howard pulled it back from the brink. The party had to go back to the drawing board and prepare itself for the day when the tough decisions which had been continuously postponed could no longer be ignored. The Iraq war had done much to destroy trust in the Prime Minister. The public felt increasingly alienated: managed but not represented.

Gordon Brown replaced Tony Blair. He came across in office as being by nature more a commissar from the old Eastern Europe than a user friendly politician. At Prime Minister's Questions he appeared to be a disaster. Attempts to replace him were not carried through and he seemed to rely on blaming the bankers for the increasingly desperate state of the economy.

Widespread misuse of parliamentary expenses when exposed led to growing contempt for politicians. When the election came no political party felt that the electorate could be trusted with the truth about how dire our economic situation had become and the pain that recovery must involve.

David Cameron had worked hard to remodel the Conservative Party. How this would now perform would be tested.

Jack Straw, when asked on a BBC 'Hardtalk' programme to name the greatest achievement of his generation of Labour politicians replied, 'The destruction of deference'. We reap what we sow, sometimes it may be the whirlwind.

Lord Derby thought it a greater honour to be Lord Mayor of Liverpool than Prime Minister. The glory days of the town hall are now distant memories but how to restore power and responsibility to local communities remains an issue as important as ever it was. Westminster is at risk of passing the same way as it is sucked dry by Brussels.

From where is a new generation of parliamentarians to come that is not content to stay on message and dares to challenge the short term and often trivial concerns of the media? That demonstrates that it is still possible to conduct debate of real quality and respect the outcome and which faces the hard issues of tomorrow?

Isaiah Berlin, in his famous monograph on leadership, 'The Fox and the Hedgehog' contrasts two styles, Rupert of the Rhine always leading the charge and once too often leaving the battlefield and losing the war and Kutuzov the Russian Commander who understood that the only thing that would beat Napoleon was the Russian winter. In today's media world to hang on to the core truth calls for exceptional qualities. Rupert would have been a hero and Kutuzov a coward as he withdrew his forces all the way to Moscow.

The ultimate challenge to any incoming Prime Minister is to find a credible answer to Dean Acheson, former American Secretary of State's jibe that Britain had lost an empire but failed to find a role. After he left office he visited Cambridge and I remember a particular evening when he spoke remarkably freely in the rooms of a friend in King's. He conceded that Roosevelt had got things wrong at Yalta in backing Stalin rather than Churchill. When Ambassador Kennan was appointed to Moscow he went with high hopes that he could establish a special relationship. The Russians gave him a statue of an eagle which sat on his desk. It contained a microphone and for almost a year everything that was said in his office went straight through to the NKVD. Acheson said that when this was discovered Kennan had to be recalled. He could not think what to do with him so he sent him on a fact-finding mission through South America. He thought nothing more about him until just before the presidential election when one of his aides came in and said, 'Secretary of State, have you read Ambassador Kennan's report?' 'No,' he said, 'should I?' The aide replied, 'Perhaps I should read the last line to you – "'who let these guys down from the trees anyway?'"' There were fifty copies in circulation. Forty-nine were located but he spent nervous days praying that the missing one would not pop up in the wrong place.

Then, as now, a gaffe resonates with the media and beyond them with the public far more loudly than any policy. It puts them back in control.

Most Americans have little knowledge of history. Indeed Henry Ford memorably described it as bunk. Whenever I was in Boston the famous Tea Party came to mind. The pig headedness of George III and the incompetence of Lord North led to the British Colonists' rebellion and their loss to the Empire. The French came in on their side, bankrupted themselves and had to live through their own particularly bloody revolution. When I ask an American would they have had their own even more bloody civil war if they had remained within the Empire and accepted the abolition of slavery from Westminster, most of them look blank. American hostility to the British Empire has been a major factor in its decline and fall.

Epilogue

To everything there is a season, and a time to every purpose under heaven:

A time to be born, and a time to die . . .

Ecclesiastes 3:1

A T THE END OF LIFE the answers to fundamental questions of our existence seem to most of us no clearer than they were at the beginning. We perhaps acquire a different perspective but one human lifetime is a pathetically short period from which to form a judgement on its relevance to the scheme of things.

Some years ago my son, Mark, who was working in the Smithsonian in Washington on the mapping of Venus took me to see a film on a huge screen in the Museum of Air and Space. It began with Galileo ascending in a balloon from St Mark's Square in Venice. The speed of lift-off was exponential and within moments we were outside the earth's atmosphere and heading ever deeper into space. Those despairing words of the blind Milton came into my mind:

> For who would lose,
> Though full of pain, this intellectual being . . .
> To perish rather, swallowed up and lost
> in the wide womb of uncreated night,
> Devoid of sense and motion?

Paradise Lost, Bk 2, 1.146

Mark told me that he had been taken by his team leader to the Pentagon. During the coffee break a Four Star General had come up and said, 'Say, can you find me a meteorite to nuke?'

In my lifetime man's capacity to destroy civilization in moments has been amply demonstrated. Over a rather longer period unrestrained population growth carries the same threat, but also in my lifetime discoveries from the secrets of DNA to those of the internet, unimaginable to previous generations, have become facts of life.

For those who seek comfort, Shakespeare reminds us:

There are more things in heaven and earth . . .
Than are dreamt of in our philosophy.

That man is the measure of all things I doubt but that he will continue to reach for the stars that is something that I do not doubt.